Serial Killers

Other Books in the History Makers Series:

Serial Killers

By Allison Lassieur

Lucent Books
P.O. Box 289011, San Diego, CA 92198-9011

Library of Congress Cataloging-in-Publication Data

Lassieur, Allison, 1963–
   Serial killers / by Allison Lassieur.
      p.   cm. — (History makers series)
   Includes bibliographical references (p.   ) and index.
   Summary: Profiles the lives and atrocities of seven serial killers:
H. H. Holmes, Albert Fish, Ed Gein, Andrei Chikatilo, John Wayne
Gacy, Ted Bundy, and Jeffrey Dahmer.
   ISBN 1-56006-650-4 (lib. bdg. : alk. paper)
   1. Serial murderers—Biography—Juvenile literature.   2. Serial
murders—Case studies—Juvenile literature. [1. Serial murderers.
2. Serial murders.   3. Murder.]   I. Title.   II. Series: History makers.
HV6245.L263   2000
364.15'23'092273—dc21   99-33814
[B]   CIP

Printed in the U.S.A.

CONTENTS

FOREWORD

The literary form most often referred to as "multiple biography" was perfected in the first century A.D. by Plutarch, a perceptive and talented moralist and historian who hailed from the small town of Chaeronea in central Greece. His most famous work, *Parallel Lives*, consists of a long series of biographies of noteworthy ancient Greek and Roman statesmen and military leaders. Frequently, Plutarch compares a famous Greek to a famous Roman, pointing out similarities in personality and achievements. These expertly constructed and very readable tracts provided later historians and others, including playwrights like Shakespeare, with priceless information about prominent ancient personages and also inspired new generations of writers to tackle the multiple biography genre.

The Lucent History Makers series proudly carries on the venerable tradition handed down from Plutarch. Each volume in the series consists of a set of six to eight biographies of important and influential historical figures who were linked together by a common factor. In *Rulers of Ancient Rome*, for example, all the figures were generals, consuls, or emperors of either the Roman Republic or Empire; while the subjects of *Fighters Against American Slavery*, though they lived in different places and times, all shared the same goal, namely the eradication of human servitude. Mindful that politicians and military leaders are not (and never have been) the only people who shape the course of history, the editors of the series have also included representatives from a wide range of endeavors, including scientists, artists, writers, philosophers, religious leaders, and sports figures.

Each book is intended to give a range of figures—some well known, others less known; some who made a great impact on history, others who made only a small impact. For instance, by making Columbus's initial voyage possible, Spain's Queen Isabella I, featured in *Women Leaders of Nations*, helped to open up the New World to exploration and exploitation by the European powers. Unarguably, therefore, she made a major contribution to a series of events that had momentous consequences for the entire world. By contrast, Catherine II, the eighteenth-century Russian queen, and Golda Meir, the modern Israeli prime minister, did not play roles of global impact; however, their policies and actions significantly influenced the historical development of both their own countries and their regional neighbors. Regardless of their relative importance in the greater historical scheme, all of the figures chronicled in the History Makers series made contributions to posterity; and their public achievements, as well as what is known about their private lives, are presented and evaluated in light of the most recent scholarship.

In addition, each volume in the series is documented and substantiated by a wide array of primary and secondary source quotations. The primary source quotes enliven the text by presenting eyewitness views of the times and culture in which each history maker lived; while the secondary source quotes, taken from the works of respected modern scholars, offer expert elaboration and/ or critical commentary. Each quote is footnoted, demonstrating to the reader exactly where biographers find their information. The footnotes also provide the reader with the means of conducting additional research. Finally, to further guide and illuminate readers, each volume in the series features photographs, two bibliographies, and a comprehensive index.

The History Makers series provides both students engaged in research and more casual readers with informative, enlightening, and entertaining overviews of individuals from a variety of circumstances, professions, and backgrounds. No doubt all of them, whether loved or hated, benevolent or cruel, constructive or destructive, will remain endlessly fascinating to each new generation seeking to identify the forces that shaped their world.

Seven Serial Killers

People are murdered every day. This is a sad fact of life. Friends kill friends, husbands murder wives, and students rampage through schools. At times, it seems as if murder is so common-place as to be routine.

But no matter how immune people may become to reports of murder, it doesn't stop the shiver of fear and revulsion that most feel at the words "serial killer." These words conjure up macabre images so bizarre that people have trouble comprehending them. A serial murderer is deadly, of course. His crimes are usually more heinous than most. But the most terrifying truth is that most serial killers appear normal. He might be a father, a boss, a landlord, or even the guy working at the next desk in the office.

Few serial killers have captured the public's horrified imagination like those that appear in this book. These seven killers might

Even though people are murdered every day, the news that a serial killer is loose causes a sense of fear and revulsion.

not be the most prolific or the most well-known. However, they all made an indelible mark on the public's consciousness.

H. H. Holmes, a savage killer who preyed on women, is considered by some to be the first modern American serial killer. His sensational trial in the late nineteenth century exposed some of the most horrific crimes that anyone—then or now—had ever seen.

It is believed that Albert Fish, a kidnapper, cannibal, and killer who stalked children in the early part of this century, might have molested hundreds of innocent children during his lifetime. To this day he is regarded by some as the most sexually perverted, dangerous killer that has ever lived.

Ed Gein, who killed only two women, was nonetheless a sensation. His habit of robbing graves and using body parts to make household objects repulsed the nation and forever imparted to Gein cult-legend status. His exploits formed the basis of numerous books and movies that audiences are familiar with even today.

Few Americans had heard of Andrei Chikatilo when he was captured in the then–Soviet Union in the early 1990s. Although he is still relatively obscure in the United States, Chikatilo is one of the most savage serial killers the world has ever known. His acts of gleeful cannibalism, rape, torture, and blood lust are unparalleled.

John Wayne Gacy will forever be known as the Killer Clown. The successful businessman who dressed in clown makeup for children also brutally murdered young boys. The public continues to be fascinated with Gacy in part because he epitomized the "serial killer in our midst" mythos. All the time Gacy was killing, he was a well-liked, respected member of the community.

Simply the name "Ted Bundy" can invoke images of brutally murdered girls. Although Bundy was hardly the first serial killer to capture the public's imagination, his cross-country killing rampage in the 1970s terrified the entire nation. Ted Bundy's actions set the benchmark for the image of the "dangerous stranger" and continues to instill fear in many American women.

When Jeffrey Dahmer's crimes were splashed across U.S. newspapers in the early 1990s, they seemed too horrific to be believed. This attractive, quiet man turned out to be a raging cannibalistic killer whose loneliness was so profound that the only way he could cure it was by keeping corpses by his side. Dahmer personified the evil monster that could live next door.

Although the atrocities of serial killers repulse people, there is a strange fascination with these deadly murderers. Humans have always been intrigued by the darker side of human nature, and no one embodies the darkest human impulses like a serial killer.

CHAPTER 1

What Is a Serial Killer?

It was a routine missing persons investigation. A boy named Robert Piest had disappeared from his job at a Chicago pharmacy. Robert's mother remembered that Robert had made an appointment to see a local contractor about a construction job the night he disappeared. Police got a search warrant and went to the man's home. When officers entered, the smell of decomposing bodies almost knocked them over. It was coming from a crawl space under the floor.

By the time police finished digging beneath the man's home, they had uncovered twenty-nine bodies. Four more had been dumped in a nearby river. Of the thirty-three victims, nine were never identified. The contractor? A prominent Chicago businessman named John Wayne Gacy.

What is a serial killer? At first glance, the answer to this question seems obvious. Serial killers are people who kill several, sometimes many other people. One definition of a serial killer is someone who has killed at least two people with a break in the time between the murders. But serial killers share a number of other characteristics.

Since 1800, there have been more than 150 documented cases of serial murderers in the United States alone. However, not until the 1970s did law enforcement agencies begin recognizing the unique characteristics of these kinds of murders. The term "serial killer" was coined in the mid-1970s by Robert Ressler, a former FBI agent. He recalls,

> I coined the term serial killer, now in much use. At that time, killings such as those of "Son of Sam" killer David Berkowitz in New York were invariably labeled "stranger killings." This term didn't seem appropriate to me, however, for sometimes killers do know their victims. Various other terms had also been used, but none hit the nail on the head. . . . So in my classes and elsewhere at Quantico [the FBI training facility] I began referring to "serial killers."[1]

The term "serial killer" was coined in the mid-1970s. Previously, murders like those by the "Son of Sam" (center) were called "stranger killings."

Although serial murder is fairly rare, it still presents a challenge to police departments. John Douglas, FBI agent and specialist on serial killers, estimates that between thirty and fifty serial killers are loose in America's cities and towns at any given time. Despite the fact that serial killers are more common than one might think, the nature of the crimes and the perpetrators means that pursuing them requires special training and skills.

Thirty years ago, few in law enforcement believed that serial killers were any different from those who committed other kinds of murders. Only in the last few years have people begun to suspect that a serial murderer is very different from any other kind of murderer—and from anyone else, for that matter. Gradually, law enforcement officials realized that understanding the minds of captured and convicted serial killers could help them catch others—cutting short some murderous rampages.

As a result of the need to understand serial killers and their crimes, the FBI formed a Behavioral Sciences unit. The focus of this department, established in the 1970s, is to recognize and catch serial killers. Within the FBI's Behavioral Sciences unit are two important divisions: the National Center for the Analysis of Violent Crime (NCAVC) and the Violent Criminal Apprehension Program (VICAP). The purpose of these divisions is to discover why serial killers commit their crimes. The agents who work in this unit use the information gleaned from dozens of interviews with convicted serial killers and hundreds of murder investigations to predict what conditions might cause someone to become a serial killer. A further role for the Behavioral Sciences unit is to aid other law enforcement agencies in solving serial crimes.

One of the biggest obstacles that police face in investigating a possible serial murder is lack of information. Many serial murderers live, and often commit their crimes, in small towns where police departments are unaccustomed to handling murder investigations—and certainly not one that could be a serial murder. The NCAVC was designed to help police anywhere in the United States or abroad deal with such shocking, violent crimes. When a community of any size is faced with a possible serial murder, the NCAVC provides training, research, and support to local police departments.

Sometimes the problem that small law enforcement departments face is recognizing a serial murder in the first place. Most police officers simply are not trained to spot the vital clues at a crime scene that would mark a murder as a serial killing. Also, many killers travel across state lines or even to other nations, killing as they go. VICAP is a nationwide data information center founded in 1985. It attempts to track this type of criminal nation-

An FBI crime analyst enters details about an unsolved murder into the VICAP data information center. VICAP allows law enforcement agencies across the nation to share evidence on violent crimes.

ally by matching cases that could be linked to the same individual. Law enforcement agencies input details about their unsolved murders into the VICAP computers. The computer matches the details with any other cases in the database, and police officers can then compare the crimes to see if they have a serial murderer on their hands. Many times, they do.

"Normal" vs. Serial Murder

At first glance, few people could see any differences between a "normal" murder and one committed by a serial killer. But there are distinct differences. Most murders are committed by people who have a specific motive for killing someone. These criminals usually have an opportunity to commit murder and the means to commit the crime. This does not necessarily mean that the crime was planned; many of these murders are committed on the spur of the moment, in anger or frustration.

For police, finding a "normal" murderer is simplified by the fact that a vast majority of these criminals kill someone they know. Investigating officers can contact witnesses, speak to family members of the victim or the suspect, and reconstruct the crime using real and circumstantial evidence.

Serial murders, on the other hand, are much more complex. Missing persons cases or abductions that end in murder can be one clue that a serial killer is at work. A murder that appears to be random, motiveless, or sexually motivated is also a clue.

Several factors add to the difficulty of investigating serial murders. Serial killers tend to plan their deeds carefully, and therefore leave fewer clues at the scene of the crime. Most serial murderers kill strangers; the police have no network of the victims' friends, acquaintances, or family members that would comprise a pool of suspects. Finally, many serial murderers kill their victims miles away from their own homes and dispose of the bodies in carefully selected locations, making it much more difficult to link them to the murder. Ted Bundy, for example, sometimes chose his dumping locations even before he chose his victims.

Mass vs. Serial Murder

There are those who kill multiple victims but who are not classified as serial murderers. These so-called mass murderers kill a large number of victims, but they do so at once, with no distinction among the victims. As is true of "ordinary" killers, the mass murderer displays some kind of motive, whether it is rage at his family, anger at an employer, or some twisted political agenda.

But unlike a serial killer, a mass murderer usually uses large weapons, such as semiautomatic weapons or bombs, in committing the crime. Timothy McVeigh, convicted of bombing Oklahoma City's Murrah Federal Building, is considered to be a mass murderer, for example. Finally, unlike serial killers, many mass murderers commit suicide immediately after their crime, putting an immediate end to their rampages.

Characteristics of a Serial Murderer

When a serial murderer such as Jeffrey Dahmer or Ted Bundy is captured, it is shocking that these men look, to most observers at least, like anyone else. However, while most serial killers look normal to casual observers, mentally they are significantly different. Over the years, the FBI's Behavioral Sciences unit has identified some specific characteristics of a serial killer. Although individual serial killers may display only some of these traits, it is clear that such murderers have many things in common.

Almost all serial killers have very active, violent fantasy lives. Many serial killers report having had killing fantasies from the time they were small children. Over the years, these violent fantasies—usually sexual in nature—become more and more real to the killer. Since it usually takes years for a killer's fantasies to overpower him, most serial murderers tend to be in their twenties and thirties. The distinction between fantasy and reality begins to blur at about that time. At some point, the fantasies of death take over and the killing begins.

Because of these fantasies, most serial murderers are incapable of having normal relationships with other people, especially women. Some killers have reported that real relationships just do not live up to the fantasies in their minds.

An overwhelming majority of serial killers are white males. Occasionally there are female serial killers, many of whom tend to have murdered a succession of husbands or lovers. Others are sometimes nurses who perform a string of "mercy killings" on patients in their care. The one thing that separates female serial killers from male, however, is the violent sexual nature of the killings. As author Harold Schechter notes,

> One of the hotly-debated issues among criminologists is whether there is such a thing as a *female* serial killer. Without a doubt, there are many women who fit the loosest definition. . . . What the crimes of such fatal females lack, however, is an element that makes the deeds of Jack the Ripper, Jeffrey Dahmer, John Wayne Gacy, etc., so pro-

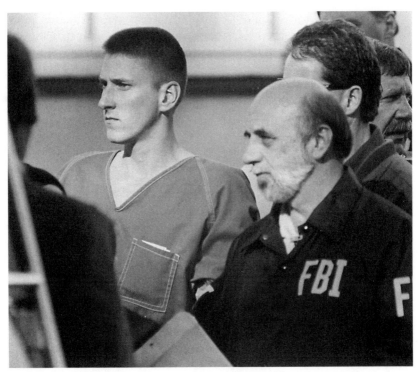

Convicted Oklahoma City bomber Timothy McVeigh is considered a mass murderer rather than a serial killer because he killed a large number of people at one time, with no distinction among the victims.

foundly nightmarish, an element of unspeakable sexual sadism. According to many experts, true serial homicide always involves the savage violation and mutilation of the victim's body.[2]

Not only do serial killers' crimes show similar characteristics, but their victims also display striking similarities. A serial killer's victims are usually women, children, or anyone who is not in a position to put up a struggle. A serial murderer is also likely to kill within his own ethnic group. An exception to this rule was Jeffrey Dahmer, a white man who killed black, Native American, Hispanic, and Asian victims. Although a serial killer usually does not know his victims, a serial killer might choose people who share particular attributes. Ted Bundy, for example, usually killed young women who had long hair parted in the middle. This peculiarity of serial killers is one of the strongest clues for investigators trying to link murders to one serial killer.

A serial killer is methodical and purposeful in committing the murders. He usually builds up the fantasy of the killing, carefully

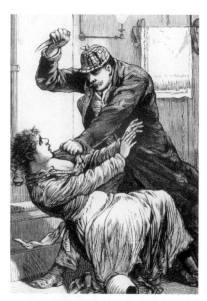

Serial homicides, such as the gruesome crimes of Jack the Ripper, involve the savage violation and mutilation of the victim's body.

planning it to perfection, before he strikes. Once a serial killer has begun his rampage, the killings are usually separated by a cooling-off period, which can last anywhere from a few hours to a few years. During this cooling-off period, almost every serial killer experiences a sense of depression because the actual crime is never as satisfying as the one in his fantasies. Most of the time this depression only motivates the killer to kill again. He begins to plan the next kill.

Most serial killers also share several characteristics in their backgrounds. Almost all convicted serial killers were abused as children. Most of the abuse was violent, many times at the hands of an alcoholic or mentally ill parent. Many of the killers began experimenting with murder as children, by torturing or killing animals. For instance, as a teen, Jeffrey Dahmer would drive around his hometown, looking for stray dogs to run over. Some committed arson in the community. Almost all of them were bed wetters until they were almost teenagers. These last three characteristics—animal torture, arson, and bed-wetting—are so common among known serial killers that law enforcement officials call them the "Triad."

As a group, serial murderers tend to be smart. Although many serial killers showed deviant behavior as children, most are of above average intelligence. However, because of their harsh upbringings or feelings of self-loathing, many of these killers cannot function well in society. Despite their intelligence, they usually end up working in boring, unsatisfying jobs that they feel are beneath them.

Occasionally, however, a serial killer will seem to be a well-adjusted, productive member of society. For example, John Wayne Gacy was so active in Chicago politics that he once had his photo taken with then–First Lady Rosalynn Carter, and Ted Bundy was successful as a college student. Regardless of these outward appearances, however, they shared the same violent fantasies as other serial murderers.

In almost all cases, serial killers tend to have large egos and a sense of invincibility. Once the killer gets away with a murder or two, he begins to believe that he will never get caught. He starts believing that the authorities are inept and stupid. Sometimes the killer will even volunteer to help with an investigation, taking on tasks such as handing out missing person fliers of his victims. Others enjoy taunting the police with letters, phone calls, and messages left at crime scenes.

Characteristics of a Serial Crime

Not only do serial killers show specific characteristics in their personality and upbringing, but their crimes display a common pattern. The most important characteristic of a serial murderer's crime is that it is usually part of an elaborate sexual fantasy that climaxes at the moment he kills. In his fantasies, the killer dreams of overpowering his victims, controlling them, and using them for his own perverse pleasures.

Arson investigators survey the aftermath of a fire. A history of committing arson is one part of the "Triad" of characteristics shared by serial killers.

Part of a serial killer's fantasy is to be as close to the victim, both physically and emotionally, as he can get. For this reason, a serial killer rarely uses guns to kill. Instead, he prefers to use more "personal" weapons, such as knives, clubs, and bare hands. Because he is so often incapable of having normal, intimate relationships, he uses his victims as physical substitutes for girlfriends, wives, or lovers.

After the killing, a serial killer usually violently mutilates the bodies of his victims. Many serial killers rape or sodomize their victims before—and after—they are dead. A few killers cannibalize their victims. Evidence of these gruesome acts at a crime scene gives law enforcement officials a strong clue that a serial killer is at work.

Serial murderers rarely use guns to kill. Instead, they prefer "personal" weapons such as knives, which allow them to get close to their victims.

Law enforcement officials who study and interview serial killers have discovered that many serial killers had very specific reasons behind such violent mutilation. Some killers remove parts of their victim's bodies as "trophies" of their crimes. Others take photographs of their victims' bodies. They use these grotesque mementos to relive their fantasies long after the crime is committed.

Sometimes the killer takes objects such as jewelry or clothing from his victims as souvenirs. When police searched John Wayne Gacy's home, for example, they found dozens of personal items, such as clothing, jewelry, and drivers' licenses, belonging to his victims.

No matter how hard local authorities and the FBI try, or how many serial murderers they catch, no one can completely explain what goes on in the mind of a serial killer. The events in a serial killer's past are things that many people face every day: abuse, violence, loneliness, low self-esteem. Thousands of people survive worse circumstances and never become serial killers. So why these few? It is unlikely that anyone will ever know for sure. But what is known is that men like Jeffrey Dahmer, John Wayne Gacy, and Ted Bundy are not fictional characters from books or television shows. They are real people with real life stories.

CHAPTER 2

The Torture Doctor: H. H. Holmes

In the summer of 1893, the grand World's Columbian Exposition opened its doors. Built on a former swamp on the shores of Lake Michigan in Chicago, the six-hundred-acre park of dazzling white buildings, exotic foods, and breathtaking rides overwhelmed all who were lucky enough to see it.

Local newspapers were filled with notices advertising accommodations for the fair. One was an ad for rooms in a building in Englewood, a suburb of Chicago. The proprietor, a successful druggist and entrepreneur named H. H. Holmes, dubbed it his "World's Fair Hotel." No one knows how many eager tourists answered Holmes's ad and stayed in his hotel. But according to some reports, more than fifty people who stayed at Holmes's World's Fair Hotel were never seen alive again.

But H. H. Holmes, also known to history as the Torture Doctor, had been very busy long before that.

Opening in the summer of 1893, the dazzling white buildings of the World's Columbian Expedition overwhelmed all who were lucky enough to see them.

Holmes's Early Years

Holmes, whose real name was Herman Mudgett, was born in 1860 in New Hampshire. Details of his early life are sketchy, but it is known that his father believed in strict discipline and frequently whipped the young Herman. His mother rarely intervened during these punishments. Herman grew to despise both parents and longed to escape small-town life.

Despite the harsh home life, Herman excelled at school. He realized early on that education would be his ticket to a better life. But Herman was teased for being smart. Older boys told horrifying stories about the village doctor, whose eerie office contained a skeleton. Author Harold Schechter describes how the doctor's office affected Herman:

> Emanating from the gloomy interior were sharp, medicinal odors, associated in little Herman's mind with the vile nostrums he was forced to imbibe whenever he was ill . . . because of certain dark stories he had heard from his schoolmates (according to rumor, the doctor's cabinets housed a collection of preserved human heads and amputated limbs) the office had assumed a terrifying dimension in little Herman's imagination.[3]

One day, some of the older boys waited until the doctor was gone, then carried the screaming Herman to the doctor's door and pushed him toward the terrible skeleton. The doctor soon returned, however, and angrily threw the bullies out of his office.

Years later, Holmes would recall this incident as the thing that created his interest in anatomy. By the time he was eleven, Holmes was performing experiments on small animals. Sometimes he kept special trophies, such as a paw or bones, from his experiments.

When Herman was only sixteen years old he became a teacher. His ambition was to save enough money to eventually go to medical school. Inexplicably, just as he'd saved enough to leave town for good, he married Clara Lovering, a local girl he'd known since childhood.

But marriage didn't slow down Herman or his plans. He soon left Clara and moved to Vermont to attend medical school. Eventually he transferred to the University of Michigan School of Medicine, never again returning to New Hampshire to live.

Holmes's Early Criminal Career

Sometime during Herman's years in Michigan he assumed the name of H. H. Holmes. In later years he would use a number of different aliases, but this one would always be his favorite. As H. H. Holmes, he committed his first known crime while he was a student at the University of Michigan. Needing money, Holmes hit upon a foolproof idea: insurance fraud. He took out a life insurance policy under a fake name and made himself the beneficiary. Then he stole a corpse from the university morgue, destroyed its face with acid, and dumped it.

In the meantime, he notified police that a friend of his was missing. When the body of his "friend" was found, police asked Holmes to identify the remains. Once he'd made a positive identification, Holmes submitted a claim to the insurance company and was delighted when the company promptly paid. From that point on, whenever Holmes needed cash in a hurry, he knew how to get it.

H. H. Holmes, also known as the Torture Doctor, committed his first crime—insurance fraud—while he was a student at the University of Michigan.

The Death Doctor Moves to Chicago

Holmes graduated from medical school in 1884. Two years later, in 1886, Holmes moved to Chicago and got a job as a druggist. Soon he acquired his own pharmacy. But Holmes was always planning get-rich-quick schemes, and he soon hit on a grand idea: marriage. Myrta Belknap was smart and pretty, but her greatest asset—as far as Holmes was concerned—was that she came from a family with money. Myrta never suspected that Holmes was already married, and she adored her dashing new husband.

At first, the couple seemed happy. But Holmes's habit of openly flirting with female customers began to wear on Myrta. He also tried swindling money from Myrta's relatives, but was caught trying to forge a check. The marriage fell apart. About this time Myrta discovered she was pregnant and moved in with her parents. Although Holmes provided for her, they never lived together again. Myrta was one of the lucky ones: she was one of the few women in Holmes's life who survived.

The Castle

Holmes now set to work on his dream: constructing his very own building. Although he had no money, he managed to pull off a number of swindles, cheating local businessmen out of goods, to raise the funds. For example, he would rent a wagonload of expensive furniture from one store, then sell it to another store across town. Soon he was able to buy a plot of land right across the street from his drugstore. Not long after that, ads for construction help appeared in local papers.

One of the men he hired, Ben Pietzel, became Holmes's right-hand man and closest confidant. Pietzel was a devoted family man with a wife and five children: Dessie, Alice, Howard, Nellie, and the baby Wharton. Ben, however, was an alcoholic. It was easy for the dapper entrepreneur to convince the drunken family man to be an accomplice to many of his illegal deals.

When completed, the impressive Holmes's Hotel was a dark building with round turrets on each corner and battlements along the roof. Townspeople dubbed it "The Castle," and the name stuck. Unknown to everyone, the Castle had some unusual features. The first and third floors were typical of buildings of the day, with offices, shops, and other rooms. The second floor, however, was different. Dimly lit, narrow hallways snaked in all directions. There were secret passageways, false doors, secret stairways, sliding walls, trapdoors, and mysterious hidden chutes. Most rooms had tiny hidden gas pipes running into the rooms, with the master control in Holmes's bedroom. Some of the rooms were soundproof. Almost all of them locked from the outside.

Women Begin to Disappear

Soon the Castle was bustling with eager merchants in the first-floor shops. One of them was a watchmaker named Ned Connor, his beautiful wife, Julia, and their two-year-old daughter, Pearl. Before long Holmes and Julia became lovers. The affair did not remain a secret, and Ned finally left. Julia and Pearl remained in Chicago. Holmes soon tired of his mistress, but Julia pressured him to marry her. When Julia became pregnant, Holmes agreed to the marriage, but only on the condition that she have an abortion, performed by him. What happened next is uncertain. But neither she nor her daughter were ever seen again.

Other women in Holmes's life disappeared as well. Gertie Connor, Ned's eighteen-year-old sister, had come to Chicago on a visit and was wooed by the dashing Holmes. She spurned his advances

Nicknamed "The Castle" by local townspeople, the Holmes Hotel had some unusual features such as secret passageways, false doors, and sliding walls, as well as soundproof rooms that locked from the outside.

and left for home, but never arrived. A few months after Julia and Gertie vanished, a stunning beauty named Emeline Cigruaud disappeared days after she and Holmes announced their wedding plans. Women who worked in the Castle, including servants, were also never heard from again.

In March of 1893 Holmes met Minnie Williams, a short, sweet Texas girl who was an heiress to a fortune. She began working for Holmes as a secretary and soon became his mistress. Holmes convinced Minnie to marry him and to sign over her money. But then Minnie heard rumors that Holmes already had a wife and made the fatal error of confronting him. In May, only two months after Minnie arrived in Chicago, Holmes invited Nannie, Minnie's sister, to visit Chicago and see the majestic exposition. Like so many before them, the two sisters were never heard from again.

During that exciting summer, a number of tourists who stayed at the Castle failed to return home. Distraught families and loved ones searched for months, but it was as if their friends and family members had simply vanished. Later, Holmes confessed to killing only one tourist, but it was suspected that he murdered dozens.

Throughout the rest of 1893 and into 1894, Holmes was a popular, successful businessman. His schemes seemed to be working

In 1893, Holmes convinced his secretary, Minnie Williams (left), to marry him and sign her fortune over to him. After her sister, Nannie (right), came to visit, neither sister was heard from again.

in his favor, and he continued to cheat anyone he could out of as much money as possible. But his world was closing in on him. The line between fantasy and reality was blurring, and it was only a matter of time before his murderous habits would catch up to him.

Holmes on the Run

On July 19, 1894, Holmes was arrested in St. Louis for fraud. At this point, his creditors in Chicago began realizing that Holmes had swindled them out of hundreds of thousands of dollars. Released on bail, Holmes fled to Philadelphia. He had already formed a new scheme, and he needed Ben Pietzel's help in carrying it out.

The scheme was another insurance fraud. Holmes would take out a $10,000 life insurance policy on Pietzel with himself as the beneficiary, then stage Pietzel's death using a substitute body. Holmes would then identify the body as Pietzel's, collect the money, and he and the Pietzel family would be rich. Pietzel's task was to find a good location where the scam could be staged. Holmes's job was to find a suitable body.

Pietzel soon found a shabby office in downtown Philadelphia that would serve as the scene for the drama to come. On Monday, September 3, 1894, a visitor to the office found the grisly remains of a body. Its face had been burned beyond recognition, the result of a small explosion.

Holmes had, indeed, found a suitable body. However, the body he had chosen was Pietzel's. In the meantime, Holmes had taken Pietzel's daughter, Alice, to Philadelphia to identify the body. Unbeknownst to everyone, he also had a new wife, Georgianna, in tow.

Alice identified her father, and the insurance company paid the claim. But because the cause of death was suspicious, they began to investigate. The pressure of the investigation sent Holmes spinning, and he got reckless. He told Mrs. Pietzel that her husband was in hiding and that he would take Alice, Nellie, and Howard to him. He soon returned to Mrs. Pietzel alone and told her that the children were safe. He would now take her to meet her husband. Holmes was now juggling three separate parties, none of which knew of the other's existence: his new wife, Georgianna; Alice, Nellie, and Howard Pietzel; and Mrs. Pietzel and the two remaining children, Dessie and Wharton.

Over the next few weeks Holmes dragged the three groups around the country. He checked into dozens of hotels, apartments, and boarding houses using different aliases. Witnesses later recalled seeing Holmes at various times either with a lady or sometimes with three children, other times with only one or two children. At the end of his flight, he had no children with him at all.

Alice Pietzel, daughter of Holmes's closest confidant, accompanied him to Philadelphia to identify her father's body. She was later found murdered, along with her sister, Nellie.

Police Arrest the Torture Doctor

The police finally caught up with Holmes in Boston. He was initially arrested for horse theft—an old charge from his Texas visit. However, when asked about Pietzel, Holmes first told authorities that Pietzel was alive. Then he remembered that no, his partner had committed suicide. He insisted that Alice, Nellie, and Howard were safe.

Gradually, the grim realization hit the police: it was likely that Holmes had killed Pietzel and his children as well as masterminding numerous frauds. Detective Frank Geyer of the Philadelphia police department was determined to find out what happened to the Pietzel children. For weeks he retraced Holmes's steps. On a hunch, he visited a lonely cottage in Toronto, Canada, that Holmes had rented at one point during his flight. The detective began digging in the cellar of the house. Author Harold Schechter picks up the story:

> Geyer had gone about a foot down when the earth gave off a carrion stench. Two feet more and he turned up a human arm bone, black with rotting flesh. . . . It took only a few moments for Geyer to uncover the bodies. . . . Alice lay on her side, with her head to the west. Nellie lay on her face, crossways to her sister, her legs resting on Alice's body. Both girls were naked.[4]

The story of H. H. Holmes burst across the nation. As more became known about the killer, other mysterious disappearances were linked to him. Every day, shocking details of Holmes and his crimes were reported in newspapers around the country. In July 1895 the *New York Times* reported:

> It is regarded as a rather uneventful day in police circles when the name of H. H. Holmes is not connected with the mysterious disappearance of one or more persons who were last seen in his company. . . . The self-confessed insurance swindler has been guilty of at least ten murders, and named the following as his victims:

> - Cigruaud, Miss, of Indiana, who was associated with Holmes for six months.
> - Connor, —, daughter of I. L. Connor. [Julia's daughter Pearl]
> - Connor, Mrs. I. L. [Julia], who left her husband for Holmes.
> - Durkey, Kate, a girl whose life Holmes insured.
> - Pietzel, Alice, found murdered in Toronto.
> - Pietzel, B. F., found dead in Philadelphia.
> - Pietzel, Nettie, found murdered in Toronto.
> - Pietzel, Howard, last seen with Holmes at Indianapolis Oct. 21, 1894.
> - Quinlan, Cora, aged 11, daughter of Janitor Quinlan, Holmes had her life insured for $1,000.
> - Williams, Annie (Nannie).
> - Williams, Minnie, sister of Annie.[5]

The Torture Castle's Horrors Discovered

The discovery of the corpses of the Pietzel girls in Toronto spurred the Chicago police to pay a visit to Holmes's building. What they found stunned them. Investigators became lost in the maze of hallways and secret rooms of the second floor. In a furnace located in Holmes's third-floor office, police discovered human bones, buttons from a woman's dress, and fragments of a lady's gold chain.

In the basement, workers found the burned remains of women's clothing and a length of bloodstained rope tied in a hangman's noose. In one corner they found acid vats and quicklime tanks. Along one wall was a contraption that looked like a medieval torture rack. In another corner of the enormous cellar sat a furnace.

When investigators searched Holmes's "Castle," they were horrified to find a contraption that resembled a medieval torture chamber, acid vats, and a bloodstained table and tools.

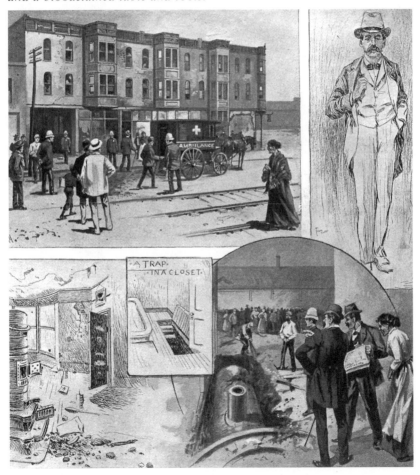

It was about two feet wide by six feet long—just large enough to hold a human body. Searchers also found a bloodstained wooden dissecting table and chests containing bloodstained surgical tools. In the middle of the basement lay a large pile of neatly stacked skeletons. Police found enough bones to reconstruct more than two hundred bodies.

On August 19, 1895, a few weeks after the police completed their investigation, a mysterious fire completely destroyed the Castle. No one was ever arrested for the fire, but the police suspected that associates of Holmes had set it to forever hide any evidence that might have remained.

"The Trial of the Century"

Despite the horrors that police discovered in Chicago, Holmes was charged only with the murder of Ben Pietzel. However, everyone

In November 1895, Holmes was convicted of murdering Ben Pietzel (pictured). Holmes was hanged on May 7, 1896.

was convinced that he had murdered hundreds more, including the Pietzel children. Holmes continued to insist that the children were alive and well, even in the face of the fact that Detective Geyer had found the Pietzel girls' remains and had also finally discovered the remains of Howard Pietzel in a house outside Indianapolis, Indiana.

Holmes's trial in Philadelphia was a circus. Reporters clamored to get close to the Torture Doctor. The evidence against Holmes was compelling. At one point, the prosecution produced a small stack of letters written by the Pietzel children. Holmes had kept them as trophies of his crimes. One, written by Alice to her grandparents, was especially heartbreaking:

> Dear Grandma and Grandpa,
>
> Hope you are well Nell and I have both got colds and chapped hands but that is all. . . . Tell Mama that I have to have a coat. I nearly freeze in that thin jacket. We have to stay in all the time now. Howard is not with us now. . . . All that Nell and I can do is draw and I get so tired of sitting that I could get up and fly almost. I wish I could see you all. I am so homesick that I don't know what to do.[6]

On November 30, 1895, after deliberating only two hours and forty-five minutes, the jury returned with the verdict: guilty of first degree murder. Herman Mudgett, alias H. H. Holmes, was sentenced to hang by the neck until dead. His execution was scheduled for May 7, 1896.

Achieving a Macabre Greatness

Following Holmes's conviction, District Attorney George Graham predicted that Holmes would confess to other crimes, saying,

> Holmes will confess fully when he finds all hope of escape gone. His pride in his criminal career is unbounded. . . . He would always cheer up when told . . . that we considered him the most dangerous criminal in the world. It is our confident belief that, before he dies, he will make such confession as will give him the highest possible rank as a wholesale criminal.[7]

The prediction proved correct. Only a month before his scheduled execution, Holmes decided to confess. Desperate to achieve some kind of macabre greatness, Holmes admitted to twenty-seven murders. Holmes spared no details in his lurid tales of murder. His favorite methods of killing, he said, were suffocation, slow starvation, gas poisoning, and burning his victims in the Castle's two large furnaces. He killed Julia's sister-in-law Gertie by substituting poison for her prescription drugs. He had suffocated Emeline Cigruaud in a huge bank vault near his office.

As for Howard Pietzel, Holmes had poisoned him and burned the body. He said he killed the Pietzel girls by forcing them into a large trunk, locking it, and filling it with gas.

By this time, however, Holmes had told so many lies that no one knew what to believe. The confession was immediately declared a sham when some of Holmes's victims turned out to be alive after all. To this day it is not clear how many people Holmes actually killed. However, despite the lingering questions, there was no slowing the approach of Holmes's execution.

The Torture Doctor Is Executed

May 7 dawned clear and calm. After a large breakfast of eggs, toast, and coffee, Holmes carefully dressed himself in a new suit and confidently climbed the scaffold. As he surveyed the crowd, he calmly claimed not to be responsible for the deaths of anyone, including Ben Pietzel and his children.

His last words made no difference. The noose was placed about Holmes's neck and the trapdoor was dropped. After Holmes was declared dead, his body was placed in a coffin, which was then filled with cement, fulfilling Holmes's last wish that his body be encased in cement, safe from grave robbers.

CHAPTER 3

The Cannibal Grandpa: Albert Fish

New York in the 1920s was an exciting place to live. Residents of Manhattan lived amid towering buildings, shops, apartment buildings, and the constant excitement of wagons, people, automobiles, trolleys, and beneath the streets, the rumble of subway trains.

To escape the oppressive New York City summers, many young men and women searched for summer jobs on country farms. The papers were filled with "Situations Wanted" notices. In May 1928 a teenager took out an ad in the *New York World*. He stated that he was eighteen and wished a position in the country. He gave his name as Edward Budd and included an address.

Across town, the ad caught the attention of an elderly man named Albert Fish. Edward did not know it, but his one-line ad, buried among dozens of others just like it, would change the life of the Budd family and eventually bring to light one of the most heinous serial killers ever known.

Fish's Early Years

Albert Fish was born on May 19, 1870, in Washington, D.C. From the start, his family was unlike any other. As many as seven of Albert's relatives were beset with severe mental illness, including a half-brother who was committed to a mental institution and an uncle who suffered from a "religious psychosis." Albert's mother claimed to hear noises and to see things. His father, Captain Randal Fish, was seventy-five years old when his son was born. Albert had an older brother who enjoyed telling his sibling stories of cannibalism in the Far East. These stories made a lasting impression on the child.

When Albert was five years old his father suddenly died, and his mother put her son in an orphanage while she looked for work. The orphanage was a place where boys suffered beatings at the hands of both the adult guardians and the other boys. Years later,

Late in life, Fish claimed that it was the brutal experience of living in an orphanage for several years that turned him into a monster.

Fish claimed that it was the brutal horrors of the orphanage that turned him into a monster. But at the time, little Albert did not always mind the punishments, and in fact came to take pleasure in the whippings administered to him. As author Moira Martingale tells it: "When one of Fish's teachers spanked the children on their bare bottoms, whereas the other infants cried, Albert Fish enjoyed it. He was only five years old at the time."[8]

After four years of this life, Fish returned home. He graduated from public school when he was fifteen and, at seventeen, began a career as a house painter. By this time the feelings of sexual pleasure that he got from inflicting pain were in full flower, and his targets—the same ones he would enjoy for the next fifty years—were children.

Fish would accept jobs in places where children gathered, such as YMCAs. He would lure a child to his basement room, then tie them up and abuse them sexually. Although it was never proved, it was suspected that Fish killed many of the children he abused. He did admit, however, to attacking both boys and girls. He preferred poor, often black children because, as he noted, the authorities at that time paid little attention when a black child was hurt or missing. By his own later admission Fish attacked between twenty-five and thirty children every year. If his claims are true, then hundreds of innocent children suffered abuse, rape, torture, and probable death at his hands.

Fish's Marriage and Family

In 1898 Fish wed a woman named Anna, nine years younger than himself, and over the course of their married life had six children. In 1917, after almost twenty years of marriage, Anna ran away with John Straube, a boarder at their home. Later, Fish would blame his wife for his crimes, claiming in a New York *Daily News* autobiography that

> The thing that started me on the real big things I have done in the last fifteen years was the trouble I had in 1917 with my wife and that man John Straube. . . . As long as Anna stuck to me and the children kept coming one after the other until there were six, I might have had my outside fancies but would keep my end of the [marriage] bargain. But when I found out about Straube, my eyes were opened to the fact that no bargains hold. . . . That freed me. It threw off my chains. I had a right after that to any fun I could find or grab.[9]

To meet children, Fish looked for work in places where they gathered, like YMCAs.

It was at about this time that Fish's odd behavior bubbled to the surface. Over the next ten years, Fish would regularly beat himself and occasionally asked his children to hit him on the buttocks with a long, nail-studded board. During the full moon, Fish would eat raw meat and demand that his children do the same. He collected newspaper articles about cannibalism and carried the yellowing clippings with him wherever he went.

This bizarre behavior was a sign of much worse things to come.

Fish Kidnaps Grace Budd

Edward Budd lived in a cramped apartment in Manhattan's Chelsea district with his father, Albert Budd, his mother, Delia, and his four siblings: Albert Jr., George, Grace, and baby Beatrice. Grace was an exceptionally pretty little girl, with huge dark eyes and short brown hair.

Edward's ad seeking work appeared in the newspaper on Sunday, May 27, 1928. On Monday, Fish appeared at the Budds' door posing as a gentleman farmer named Frank Howard. Fish dazzled the Budd family with stories about his successful farm on Long Island. Yes, he needed help. He would return to get Edward in a week.

When Fish returned to the Budd home a week later, he kept up the charade by bringing fresh strawberries and cheese "from his farm." In reality, he had just purchased them from a street vendor. He also had another bundle with him that unbeknownst to the Budds contained a butcher knife, a meat cleaver, and a small hand saw.

While Fish was in the apartment, Mrs. Budd introduced him to her daughter, Grace. As the trusting girl sat on the kindly man's lap, Fish told Grace's parents that he would be attending a family birthday party that afternoon and invited Grace to go with him. They hesitated, then agreed.

Fish and Grace boarded a train bound for the country town of Greenburgh, New York. On a quiet country road sat an empty house that the local townspeople called Wisteria Cottage. When they arrived at the house, Fish instructed Grace to stay in the yard, then he climbed the rickety stairs to the second floor. Fish removed his clothes, then called the girl upstairs.

When Grace saw the shriveled old man, she tried to run. Fish grabbed the girl and pinned her to the floor as she screamed. He knelt on the girl's chest, choking her. As Grace struggled, Fish squeezed the girl's throat until she was dead.

Fish mutilated Grace's body and carved off pieces of her flesh. After he wrapped them up in some old newspapers that he'd

After kidnapping Grace Budd, Fish took her to an empty house such as this one in Greenburgh, New York. He later strangled her and mutilated her body.

found scattered in the house, he cleaned himself off and took the train home. Once there, he made a gruesome stew, which he savored for the next nine days.

Meanwhile, the frantic Budd family had contacted the police, and one of the most sensational criminal investigations in New York history began. Photos of a smiling Grace filled the pages of newspapers all over the city. Thousands of tips poured in, but they all led nowhere. Grace and the mysterious "Mr. Howard" seemed to have vanished. It would be six years before the Budds knew the fate of their dark-eyed child.

Fish Is Captured

One detective, William King, was determined to find Grace. He never lost hope that one day the mystery would be solved. That day came on November 12, 1934. That afternoon, Edward Budd appeared at King's office and handed him a letter that had been sent to his mother. King began to read a story so vile that he could scarcely believe it. The writer first identified himself as the man who had come to the Budd house bringing strawberries and cheese. He then went on to give horrific details of the crime, including how Grace had died and been consumed by the killer.

Detective King had seen many false leads over the years, but this letter rang chillingly true. He soon traced the stationery to a rooming house in the city. For a month, King and his detectives watched the rooming house and monitored the mail. Finally, on December 13, Fish appeared. He surrendered without a struggle.

Fish Confesses to Murder

Under questioning, Fish confessed to the murder of Grace Budd. Even after King and the rest of the police department heard Fish's terrible story, and even after the city newspapers blared the gory details of Fish's crimes all over the city, few could believe it. Fish admitted that it was Edward, not Grace, that he had originally decided to kidnap. In fact, his choice of victims had been almost random. Harold Schechter writes:

> Not that he [Fish] had any animosity toward Edward Budd. He hadn't even known of the young man's existence until the morning of May 27, 1928, when he had spotted Edward's classified ad in the *New York World*. It was simply that Fish felt the need for a sacrificial victim, preferably male.[10]

Fish's plan had been to take the boy to Wisteria Cottage, tie him up, and castrate him. Fish had had no intention of killing Grace; the tools in the bundle had been meant for use on Edward. But when he saw Grace that day, he had decided to kill her instead.

Over the next few days, police swarmed over Wisteria Cottage, digging for evidence that would prove Fish's story. The searchers eventually found the rusted cleaver and saw, as well as most of Grace's small skeleton. As impossible it was to believe, Fish was telling the truth.

Fish was also subjected to a battery of psychological evaluations to determine whether he was insane. During one session Fish mentioned that he had inserted some needles into his groin as penance for killing Grace. At first the doctors were incredulous at this bizarre remark. As the details of Fish's crimes began to unfold, however, they began to take it seriously. An X ray of Fish's abdomen was ordered. It showed twenty-nine needles, shoved so far into Fish's groin and abdomen that they could not be removed. Some had clearly been lodged inside the old man for decades.

Police and the public were stunned and wondered why anyone would do such a thing. Fish calmly explained that certain "feelings" would come over him, and they would compel him to stick needles in his body. Fish added that when he was unable to stick them in himself he enjoyed torturing other people with them.

Fish on Trial

The press had a field day with the Fish trial. Daily, the residents of New York were greeted with such lurid newspaper headlines as "Fish's Weird Acts Told By Children," and "'Not in Right Mind,' Fish Wrote to Son." During the trial it was revealed that for years, Fish had sought out lonely women through marriage services, similar to modern-day dating services. He enjoyed writing these women violent, obscene letters.

One psychiatrist explained that Fish suffered from religious delusions. Fish claimed that Christ had visited him and told him He wanted Fish

Police search for clues near Wisteria Cottage. Six years after the crime, Fish confessed to the murder of Grace Budd after being captured by police.

to sacrifice a virgin so that she would not become a prostitute. At Fish's trial, his oldest daughter, Anna Collins, recounted a strange incident with her father that was also laced with religious overtones.

> When she had discovered her father sleeping . . . rolled up in a carpet on the living room floor of their home in Elmsford, New York, in 1917, he replied to her questions that "St. John the Apostle told me to do it." Mrs. Collins declared her father left her residence in March 1928, a few months before the Budd murder. Asked why he was going, he replied, "God told me to leave."[11]

Although much of Fish's behavior was described by the defense as insane, the jury did not agree. They returned a verdict of sane and guilty of first-degree murder. The judge then decreed that Fish would die by electrocution. When he got the news, Fish waved at the judge and heartily thanked him.

Albert Fish meets with his attorney. Despite defense claims that he was insane, Fish was found guilty of first-degree murder and sentenced to die in the electric chair.

After the verdict, reporters swarmed around Fish, eager to record every gesture for the morning papers. The papers quoted him as saying, "What a thrill it will be to die in the electric chair! It will be the supreme thrill—the only one I haven't tried!"[12]

Following his trial, Fish confessed to earlier crimes, in the process closing two cases that had baffled authorities for years. Fish admitted that in 1924 he had lured eight-year-old Francis McDonnell into the woods near the boy's home on Staten Island and strangled him. Fish also confessed to having kidnapped four-year-old Billy Gaffney as he was playing near his parents' Brooklyn apartment and tortured and killed the child. Fish then mutilated and cannibalized the little boy's body.

The Execution of Albert Fish

Police officers led Fish toward the electric chair on Thursday, January 16, 1936. The officers strapped Fish into the chair and attached the electrodes to his body and shaven head. Then the executioner flipped the switch.

Over the years, sensational stories have claimed that the needles in Fish's body short-circuited the chair, forcing the executioners to electrocute Fish twice. Some accounts described showers of blue sparks that flew from Fish's body when the chair was activated. Other eyewitness accounts, however, insist that Fish died with no drama or excitement.

Regardless of the stories, at around 11 P.M. doctors declared Fish to be dead. He was buried quietly and soon forgotten by almost everyone. But if even part of Fish's horrible confessions and the crimes they depict are true, Fish remains one of the most prolific sex criminals and killers of all time.

CHAPTER 4

The Monster That Movies Are Made Of: Ed Gein

The south-central plains area of Wisconsin in the 1950s could be a lonely place. Miles of flat farmland stretched to the horizon, broken only by the occasional barbed wire fence or forgotten dirt road. Small farm towns dotted the countryside.

Plainfield, Wisconsin, was just such a place. The hardworking people who lived in Plainfield took care of their own. Even a quiet, lonely handyman like Ed Gein could always find honest work and a friendly kitchen table where he could share a home-cooked meal.

As the townsfolk went about their lives, no one gave much thought to the shy little man with the cold eyes who lived all alone in a ramshackle farmhouse outside of town. He was free to do whatever he wanted. And what Ed Gein wanted became the stuff of nightmares.

Gein's Early Life

Ed Gein was born August 27, 1906, to George and Augusta Gein. George, an alcoholic, was completely dominated by his over-bearing wife. When Ed was born the Gein family owned a general store, and Augusta was the owner. Ed also had an older brother, Henry. At first, Augusta was bitterly disappointed that both her children were boys. But she resolved that these boys would grow up to be good, God-fearing men, if she had anything to do with it.

Even as a youngster, Ed understood that Augusta was the powerful one in the family. One childhood incident made a deep impression on the boy. Behind the Gein's store was a mysterious shed, where Gein's parents forbade him to go. Once, when his curiosity got the better of him, little Ed crept to the shed and peeked in the door. His parents were inside, slaughtering a hog that was hanging from a chain in the ceiling. Biographer Harold Schecter depicted the scene this way:

> His mother slipped a long-bladed knife down the length of its belly, pulled open the flaps, reached inside, and began to work at the glistening ropes of its bowels, which slid out of the carcass and into a large metal tub at her feet. Both of his parents had on long leather aprons spattered with blood. He must have made some sort of noise, because his mother turned to look at him.
>
> For the rest of his life he remembered the moment

Although Ed Gein (right) was first arrested for robbing a hardware store, officers soon discovered that Gein had committed much more heinous acts.

. . . the dangling beast, its carcass split open, its guts slopping out onto the ground, his mother standing beside it, blood and slime smeared down the length of her body.[13]

When Ed was seven, the family moved to a well-kept, isolated farmstead outside Plainfield. Both boys attended school and were average students. But Augusta refused to allow her sons to make friends, and any attempt by either Henry or Ed to have a social life was immediately condemned by their mother.

As the boys grew, their home life became more difficult. George had become an abusive alcoholic and regularly beat Augusta and the boys during his drunken rages. Augusta would scream and fall to her knees, praying aloud that her husband would drop dead. As the years passed, Augusta's religious fanaticism grew. She became convinced that all women were evil. Her boys were never to associate with such vile creatures. Although Henry tried to defy his mother, he was no match for her powerful personality.

Ed succumbed to his mother's wishes and never even tried to approach the opposite sex. And Augusta got her way. Neither Henry nor Ed ever had a normal relationship with a woman their entire lives.

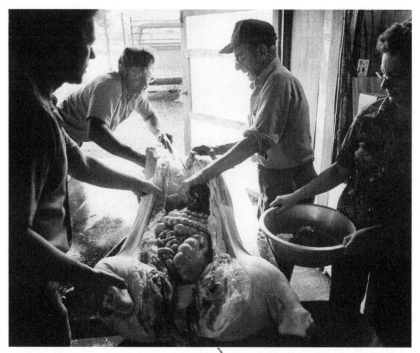

Farmers butcher a pig. Gein's childhood experience of watching his parents slaughter a pig on the family's farm made a lasting impression on him.

Tragedies for Gein

In 1940, George Gein, by now an invalid in need of constant care, died. The farm was failing. To make ends meet, both Gein brothers, now middle-aged men, started working as handymen around town. Three years after George's death, Henry died in a fire on the Gein farm. According to Ed Gein, Henry was consumed by a brush fire while Gein was trying to get the flames under control.

Gein's story had some odd inconsistencies. For one thing, Gein was able to take a search party directly to Henry's body, although he had said that he had lost track of his brother. Henry also had some mysterious bruises on his head. However, the coroner determined that Henry had been overcome with smoke and had hit his head on a rock. The case was closed.

Soon after they buried Henry, Augusta suffered a stroke. For months, Gein cared for his bedridden mother and prayed for her recovery. Only a year after the first stroke, however, Augusta died of a second one. Gein was devastated by the loss of the only person in the world who cared for him. He was now completely alone.

Gein's Nighttime Crimes

After his mother's death, Gein seemed no different, at least on the outside. He continued to work at odd jobs around town, returning home each evening to the lonely farm in the Wisconsin countryside. But something was definitely not right with Ed Gein. Gein began to hear his mother's voice talking to him. He imagined that he saw faces in piles of leaves around the farm. He became convinced that he could raise the dead through sheer willpower.

With this newfound imagined power, Gein traveled to Augusta's grave constantly, trying to bring his mother back again with his mind. But no matter how much he begged his beloved Augusta to return from the grave, he remained alone.

These graveside visits gave Gein another idea. Over the next five years, starting in 1947, Gein visited cemeteries and dug up the recently buried bodies of middle-aged women. Many of them bore a striking resemblance to his mother. Sometimes he took the bodies home with him.

Once he returned to his house with a corpse, Gein would mutilate it, using various parts as materials for bizarre crafts projects.

After his mother's death, Gein started digging up recently buried bodies of middle-aged women. Many of the women resembled his mother.

Pieces of skin, for example, became book covers or window shades. But Gein's prized possession was the most ghastly of all his creations. He sewed together a vest made of a woman's breasts and torso that he could wear. Sometimes, late at night, Gein would put on his hideous costume and wander around his house.

Gein's Fantasies Take Over

Eventually, dead bodies failed to satisfy Gein. He needed someone fresher to work with. That someone turned out to be a Plainfield woman named Bernice Worden. Worden was a stout, middle-aged hardware store owner. By all accounts she was a shrewd business-woman and a respectable person. But somehow Gein convinced himself that she was just like the evil women Augusta had always warned him to avoid.

Saturday, November 16, 1957, was the height of the deer-hunting season, and the town was practically deserted. Gein went into Worden's store to buy antifreeze. When the woman turned her back, Gein shot her with a .22, then dragged her body outside to his truck and drove away.

Later that afternoon Worden's son Frank came into the store and saw the cash register missing. When he looked closer, he no-ticed blood on the floor. He immediately thought of Gein, who had been spending a lot of time in his mother's store. Frank noti-fied the local sheriff, and officers arrested Gein as a robbery sus-pect. As Gein was being transported to the city jail, a group of men assembled in town. In the cold, dark November night, they all drove out to Gein's farm.

When they arrived, the house was dark and empty. Although the doors were locked, someone noticed that a door to the sum-mer kitchen was open. The men pushed their way inside, and their flashlights lit up something in front of them. Hanging upside down by a chain from the roof was a white, stiff carcass. It had been butchered in the same way a deer or other game animal would have been. But this was no deer. It was Bernice Worden.

Soon a large group of officers had gathered at Gein's house. Slowly, the group entered the main house. In the eerie glow of kerosene lamps and flashlights (Gein's house had no electricity) the men saw that Gein's house was unlike any they'd ever seen. The kitchen was piled high with rotting food, piles of newspapers and magazines, old cans, bottles, tools, rags, discarded clothing, cardboard boxes, and overturned furniture.

One officer, peering closely at a chair, saw that the woven cane seat had been replaced with strips of human skin. On the table sat

When police officers searched Gein's house, they found the kitchen filled with rotting food, old newspapers, and discarded clothing.

a bowl fashioned from a human skull. An oatmeal box held four noses. Almost everywhere they looked, officers found something even more horrible. Biographer Harold Schecter notes:

> One of the most bizarre things in Gein's house was his mask collection. . . . The masks were actually human facial skins that had been painstakingly peeled from the skulls of nine women. They had no eyes, of course, just holes where the eyes had been. . . . Some of them still had lipstick on their mouths and looked quite lifelike. . . . Four of these face-skins had been stuffed with paper and hung on a wall of Ed's bedroom like hunting trophies.[14]

In sharp contrast to the filth of the kitchen, searchers were astounded when they opened up a sealed door and saw Augusta's parlor, dusty but still as neat as the day she died. Gein had kept this shrine to his mother all these years. The men had seen enough. They returned to the jail where Gein was being held and informed him that he was being charged with murder.

Gein Confesses to Grisly Crimes

Gein told investigators the story of how he had murdered Worden. He insisted that he was in a "daze" the entire time, a state that had come over him frequently after his mother had died.

Investigators asked Gein where the body parts in his house had come from, thinking that he must have murdered more women. The officers were even more horrified when Gein calmly described in detail how he robbed graves. In addition to telling about his grave-robbing activities, Gein also confessed to the murder of another woman, Mary Hogan, who had disappeared some time before.

At first, no one could figure out why Gein would do such horrific things. Slowly, however, they discovered that Gein was consumed with an unnatural attachment to his mother. His one desire had been to be just like her, to the point that he would don the masks and the vest so that he could transform himself into a

After his arrest in 1957, Gein (far right) described how he had murdered Bernice Worden. He also confessed to killing another woman, Mary Hogan, some time before.

woman. All of Gein's grotesque activities were part of his desperate desire to please his mother and bring her back from the dead.

Investigators decided the only way to find out whether Gein was telling the truth was to open some of the graves he claimed to have robbed. A few months after Gein was arrested, searchers dug into one grave that Gein had pointed out. The coffin was empty. Gein had been telling the truth.

Gein Is Committed to a Mental Hospital

From the time Gein was arrested, he had been subjected to psychological testing. Doctors poked, probed, and examined Gein for days. Although Gein was of average intelligence, doctors found him emotionally stunted. He had trouble forming relationships and expected everyone else to conform to his rigid beliefs. As with many serial killers, Gein blamed his troubles on everyone but himself. He told one doctor that he would never have gotten into trouble if he had gotten married or if his neighbors had somehow treated him better.

At Gein's official sanity hearing on January 6, 1958, doctors testified that Gein was a chronic schizophrenic who lived in his own fantasy world. Although Gein did have some idea of right and wrong, his judgment was severely impaired by his mental illness. Some of the doctors had to admit that his behavior was beyond their comprehension. The judge agreed. He declared Gein legally insane and committed him to a mental institution.

Gein's House Is Consumed in Flames

Because of legal bills, it was decided that the Gein property would be auctioned off. Notices appeared in the papers. But the night before the auction was to take place, neighbors awoke to bright red flames licking the horizon in the direction of Gein's farm. The house and its contents burned to the ground.

Despite the fire, however, the auction went on as planned. Most of Gein's farm tools and other outdoor items that escaped the blaze sold for modest prices. His car, a 1949 Ford sedan, was sold to a sideshow owner by the name of Bunny Gibbons. For years afterward he exhibited Gein's "Ghoul Car" at carnivals around the country, charging twenty-five cents for a peek at "The Car That Hauled Dead From Their Graves."

Gein's Later Life

Gein spent ten quiet years in the mental hospital, happily working in the crafts shop and enjoying the company of the other patients. Eventually doctors felt that Gein was recovered enough

Gein (center) arrives at his trial after spending ten years in a mental institution. Gein was found not guilty by reason of insanity and was returned to the institution, where he spent the remainder of his life.

to understand the charges against him. Although he was still classified as insane, Ed Gein was now ready to stand trial for murder.

By the time the trial got under way on January 28, 1968, the courtroom was packed. Witnesses recounted the story of Bernice Worden's abduction and death. The judge quickly handed down the verdict: guilty of first-degree murder.

The second phase of the trial was to determine if Gein was sane at the time of the murder, and it lasted all of two hours. After the judge heard testimony, he handed down the second verdict: not guilty by reason of insanity.

The trial was the last time Gein appeared in public. He returned to the mental institution, where he died at the age of seventy-eight on July 26, 1984. A few days later, his body was transported to Plainfield, where he was secretly buried at night. Fittingly, Gein was buried beside his mother.

Gein's Life Inspires Art

In a sense, Ed Gein lives on. His story has had a powerful influence on American popular culture. A writer named Robert Bloch was living less than thirty miles away from Plainfield when the

Gein story broke. He used Gein as his inspiration for a horror novel titled *Psycho*. In 1960 film director Alfred Hitchcock released the now-famous movie based on Bloch's book.

In 1975 in Austin, Texas, a filmmaker named Tobe Hooper made *The Texas Chainsaw Massacre*, based on tales of Ed Gein he had heard as a child. And in 1991, Gein indirectly entered moviegoers' lives once again with the release of *Silence of the Lambs*. Both the sadistic serial killer Jame Gumb and the chilling Hannibal Lecter characters were based on the exploits of Ed Gein.

CHAPTER 5

Soviet Stalker: Andrei Chikatilo

The Soviet Union of 1990 was both an exciting and bleak place to live. Communism was crumbling. Soviet leader Mikhail Gorbachev was struggling to maintain control against the tide of change that his reforms had unleashed.

For the people in the Soviet province of Rostov, however, not much had changed. The concrete block buildings still had their stooped, defeated look. The trains and buses still ran late, and still stopped at makeshift stations that were little more than concrete slabs. The only thing that broke the landscape were "forest strips" that had been planted years before to prevent soil erosion. By 1990, however, these forest strips had become murder sites. Dozens of mutilated corpses had been found in the strips around Rostov, and in others throughout the region.

For years Inspector Issa Kostoev, chief of the Office of Crimes of Special Importance, had been searching for the killer. Time and time again, he had seemed so close, only to fail. But Kostoev had a feeling that, finally, the end was near.

What he would discover was only the smallest part of the story.

Chikatilo's Early Life

Andrei Chikatilo, the man who would become known as one of the Soviet Union's most heinous criminals, was born on October 16, 1936, in the village of Yablochnoye, Ukraine. By all accounts his childhood was a painful, bleak one. His older brother, Stepan, had been horribly killed before Andrei was born. His mother constantly told the story of his brother's demise at the hands of desperate, starving people. Author Richard Lourie relates the tale:

> During the great Ukranian famine of the early thirties, his older brother, Stepan, was abducted and cannibalized. It was not a unique event for those times, but that didn't take

the pain and horror out of it for Chikatilo's mother, who wept bitterly, copiously, every time she told him the story, which was often.[15]

His father, a Soviet soldier in World War II, was imprisoned in a Nazi prisoner of war camp. Following his release at the end of the war, his father was reviled as a traitor for allowing himself to be captured by the Nazis. Villagers constantly hurled insults at Chikatilo's family. One writer, Moira Martingale, tells what life was like:

> His father was to blame. . . . On his return to the Soviet Union [after the war] he was arrested again, an enemy of the people for allowing himself to be captured, was placed in a work camp far from home and regarded as an outcast because of it. His family suffered their neighbors' spite because of this . . . and the boy bore it badly.[16]

Andrei Chikatilo, known as the "Rostov Ripper," howls while listening to the judge read the verdict in his trial.

In addition to his other problems, Andrei wet his bed until he was almost a teenager and constantly complained of severe headaches. Andrei's eyesight was very bad, and he had to live with the torture of a blurred world. He also discovered early on that he was incapable of normal sexual relations. This intensified his feelings of being weak and unmanly. All of his life he bitterly believed that, at least symbolically, he had been born without eyes or genitals.

Andrei's dream was to become a lawyer, but he was furious to discover that his father's disgrace kept him from being accepted at law school. However, he eventually earned three degrees: in Russian language and literature, engineering, and Marxism-Leninism. For all outward appearances, Chikatilo seemed to be the perfect Soviet citizen and Communist Party member: hardworking, steady, and a little dull.

Chikatilo's Marriage and Family

In 1963 Chikatilo met a twenty-four-year-old beauty named Fayina and they were soon married. On their wedding night, Fayina realized that Chikatilo was unable to perform sexually. Although Chikatilo eventually managed to father two children with Fayina, they rarely had sex during their marriage.

Eventually Chikatilo became a teacher. He had also begun a career of molesting children that would last for the rest of his life. He enjoyed fondling his female students and discovered that he got sexual pleasure from their fear. It was not long before he was caught and fired. Thus began a routine that lasted for years: Chikatilo would be hired at a school, he would be caught molesting children, then he would be fired. Chikatilo eventually ended up teaching in a mining school for boys in the town of Shakhty.

The molestations were not the only activities Chikatilo's wife was unaware of. Chikatilo had purchased a shabby house in a run-down area of town. Writer Moira Martingale tells how the house was used:

> Here, he was to bring a succession of prostitutes in an effort to overcome his impotence. . . . Unlike his good, pure Fayina, these women were loose and promiscuous. They were prepared to perform sexual acts which he would never have dreamed of suggesting to Fayina.[17]

Chikatilo also brought young girls here, where their screams could not be heard. It was not difficult for Chikatilo to go undetected; the Soviet Union of the 1970s was a fearful, secretive place.

No one was inclined to investigate a child's cries coming from a run-down house in a bad part of town.

Chikatilo Begins Killing

Chikatilo's life changed on a chilly day in 1978. That afternoon, he spotted Lena Zakotnova, a pretty nine-year-old, waiting at a bus stop. He began a conversation with the girl. As they chatted, Lena confessed that she had to go to the bathroom. Chikatilo kindly offered his bathroom and explained that his house was just up the road.

As soon as they got inside the filthy house he locked the door

Although this young Soviet schoolgirl was not one of Chikatilo's victims, he did molest many of the young girls who attended the schools where he taught.

and attacked. He strangled her until she was unconscious, then attempted to rape her. Unable to complete the act, Chikatilo was overwhelmed with the urge to hurt Lena. Taking out his knife, Chikatilo stabbed the child repeatedly in the abdomen. As he did, a sense of sexual gratification flooded over him. He had finally, at age forty-two, discovered the secret to arousing his passion. One scholar who has studied serial killers, Stephen Giannangelo, writes, "After his first murder, he realized that blood aroused him and that nothing else would satisfy him sexually. He was excited by inflicting pain."[18]

He dumped the girl's body in the nearby river and went home. Chikatilo's cooling-off period lasted three years. During that time, he became a factory engineer, a position which suited him perfectly, because his new job was to visit sites throughout the region. He now had unlimited opportunities to continue his secret activities.

In 1981 he found himself in Rostov, at that time a large Soviet city. His first victim there was sixteen-year-old Larisa Tkachenko. Chikatilo led her to a park in a nearby forest strip and strangled Larisa until she was almost unconscious, then killed her with his knife, mutilating her sexual organs in the process. Nine months later Chikatilo struck again. On June 6, 1982, he led a twelve-year-old girl into the woods near a bus stop. Lyuba Biryuk's body bore what was to become a Chikatilo "signatures"—mutilated eyes. Writer Richard Lourie speculates on why he might have done this: "He may also have come to believe that there was something to the age-old superstition that the image of the murderer is imprinted on the victim's eyes. . . . No one would find his image on what was left of that girl's eyes."[19]

The monster was unleashed. For the rest of 1982, Chikatilo killed seven children and teenagers, three of them in the space of three weeks. He perfected his routine: carrying his weapons and an extra set of clothing with him at all times, watching the bus stops and train stations for possible victims, choosing a young person who seemed alone or lost, striking up a conversation.

Unlike other serial murderers, Chikatilo was not choosy about his victims. He killed boys, girls, teenagers, and young women. He performed gruesome mutilations on his victims, usually involving their sexual organs. Years later, as police tracked him, they would be amazed and repelled by Chikatilo's extreme violence.

In 1983 Chikatilo killed seven people. But in December he was caught stealing items from work and was fired. Chikatilo was furious at his dismissal and began killing with a wild frenzy. Between January and August of 1984 he butchered fourteen victims. Ten of those were killed in two months—more than one per week. On these victims, the mutilations were worse. Sometimes he built a small fire and cooked his victim's internal organs.

Chikatilo frequented the Rostov train station and bus stops looking for possible victims. He always carried his weapons and a spare set of clothing with him.

Chikatilo Eludes Capture

By 1984 the authorities in Rostov province knew they had a horrible killer on their hands. But the ever present Soviet secrecy prevented anyone from discussing the problem openly. No newspapers carried reports of the case.

In addition to the secrecy, police ineptitude and laziness enabled Chikatilo to continue his crime spree. After Lena's murder, for example, her body was found within walking distance of Chikatilo's rented house and he had been questioned by police. When police discovered that a convicted rapist also lived nearby, however, they had let Chikatilo go. The other man was eventually executed for Lena's murder.

Detectives consistently ignored suspects, misplaced files, and lost evidence. Part of the reason was the Soviet system: a huge, slow-moving bureaucracy where paperwork piled high and bribes were necessary to get even the simplest information. The system allowed Chikatilo to go free for thirteen years, killing everywhere he went.

Chikatilo was arrested once, in 1984. By that time "Operation Forest Strip" as the police called the investigation, was in full swing. Undercover officers patrolled train stations in the hopes of glimpsing the killer, and one day two officers watched the odd behavior of a tall, stooped-shouldered man. The official arrest report describes what one officer saw:

> Zanosovsky [a police officer] pointed out to me a tall man, approximately 180 cm in height, lean, about 45 years of age *whose features were very reminiscent of those in the composite sketch.* He was wearing glasses, no hat . . . carrying a brown briefcase. Zanosovsky told me that *he had seen this man before when he had been on patrol without me at the Suburban Bus Station and considered him suspicious.* . . . I was struck by his strange behavior, he seemed very ill at ease and was always twisting his head from one side to the other. . . . The suspect attempted to make contact with a girl who was standing beside him. She was wearing a low-cut dress and he couldn't take his eyes off her breasts. . . . On the bus he would stop by women and stare at them and press up against them. . . . [Emphasis added][20]

Chikatilo finally found a prostitute who agreed to have sex with him. The officers then arrested him for "licentious behavior in public" and also on suspicion for the forest strip murders. The undercover officers discovered a sharp knife, two lengths of rope, and a jar of Vaseline in his briefcase.

Chikatilo's blood was tested and found not to match the semen found at some of the crime scenes. (Later it would be discovered that Chikatilo had a rare condition in which his blood and semen did not match.) Because Chikatilo's blood did not match the semen of the "Forest Strip Killer," he was dropped as a suspect. However, officers discovered that he was still wanted in connection with the thefts from his former employer. He was sent to jail to await trial.

When his case came up on December 21, 1984, he was convicted of theft and sentenced to a year of corrective labor. But the court decided that the three months Chikatilo had already spent in jail were enough and he was set free. He would continue killing for the next six years.

The Monster Is Captured

In 1985 the KGB assigned Inspector Issa Kostoev, chief of the Office of Crimes of Special Importance, to the case. Kostoev had a reputation of solving every case he had investigated, and he had no intention of letting this murder mystery be the one that would defeat him. For six long, frustrating years Kostoev searched for the killer.

Meanwhile, Chikatilo continued to live his double life, getting another job and living quietly with Fayina and their children. By all outward appearances, Chikatilo was a quiet, dutiful husband and father. But when he was not home with his family, his killing spree went on unabated. In 1987 there were three victims, three more in 1988, five in 1989, and eight in 1990.

In the end, it was a combination of politics and plain old good luck that brought Kostoev face to face with Chikatilo. By 1990, communism's grip on the Soviet Union was loosening. With these changes came a new openness. Citizens began to hear of the terrible killer in their midst. Reports of a strange man with glasses and a briefcase approaching people at train stops began trickling in.

Then on November 6, 1990, an undercover officer watched a man wash his hands and feet at a train station. He had sticks and leaves on his clothes and a smear of something dark on his cheek. The officer dutifully noted the man's name—Andrei Chikatilo—in his logbook and promptly forgot about it. Six days later, Kostoev saw the report and hit the roof. When he read the file on Chikatilo, he was stunned by what he saw: The man had been questioned before, and had even been a suspect in the first murder. Finally, here, was a possibility.

Kostoev decided to arrest Chikatilo on suspicion of murder, but it was risky. According to Soviet law, he would have only ten days to hold Chikatilo. If Chikatilo didn't confess, he would have to be released.

Chikatilo was arrested and brought to KGB headquarters. Every day the two men talked in a small interrogation room. Every day Chikatilo denied his crimes, although he did admit to the child molestations. Every day Kostoev talked to Chikatilo, demanding answers and refusing to believe the lies. Finally, on the tenth day, Chikatilo cracked. He confessed to killing more than fifty people between 1978 and 1990.

Turning into a Beast

Over the next few days Kostoev listened in horror as Chikatilo went into graphic detail on how he mutilated still-living victims and cannibalized body parts that he removed. Chikatilo insisted that evil forces caused him to commit murder. He insisted that he turned into a wild beast and compared himself to a crazed wolf.

All together, Chikatilo confessed to fifty-five murders, some of which Kostoev had not even suspected that Chikatilo had committed.

Chikatilo's Trial and Execution

Chikatilo went on trial for murder on April 14, 1992. As soon as he entered the courtroom, he was hustled into a huge iron cage, built to keep him safe from the rage of the victims' families. During the trial, Chikatilo played the role of an insane killer to the hilt. He would scream obscenities and rattle the bars of his cage. Some days he would recant his confession, other days he would admit to new murders. Most of the time he sat, lolling his head and drooling.

After ten days of interrogation, Chikatilo confessed to killing fifty-five people between 1978 and 1990, claiming that evil forces caused him to commit the murders.

While in the courtroom, Chikatilo was kept in a huge iron cage to keep him safe from the rage of his victims' families.

Chaos reigned. Relatives of the victims fainted and had to be carried out of the courtroom during testimony. One brother of a victim hurled a metal ball at Chikatilo, barely missing him. Despite the theatrics, the horrible truth of Chikatilo's crimes could not be hidden. On October 14, 1992, the judge sentenced Chikatilo to death. A little over a year later, on February 14, 1994, Chikatilo was executed for the murders. The nightmare was over.

Chapter 6

Killer Clown: John Wayne Gacy

The 1970s was an era of change in America. The Vietnam War was over. People watched *The Waltons, Little House on the Prairie,* and *Happy Days* on television. A science fiction movie called *Star Wars* shattered Hollywood records. Disco music ruled the airwaves. And in Chicago, a successful contractor named John Wayne Gacy felt on top of the world.

By 1978 his business was thriving. He was a respected member of the community. Although he had recently divorced, he was in an upbeat mood. He had no need for a wife. He had other people who could satisfy the urges he felt, the urges that came over him late at night. When those urges overpowered him, he brought people home to 8213 Summerdale, a small, neat house in the Chicago suburb of Des Plaines.

All of them were teenage boys, and most were never seen alive again.

Gacy's Early Life

John Wayne Gacy Jr. was born in 1942 into what seemed to outsiders a solid middle-class Chicago family. His mother was a homemaker who cared for Gacy, his older sister JoAnne, and his younger sister Karen. His father, John Wayne Gacy Sr., was an alcoholic and a rigid disciplinarian. As with many serial killers, Gacy grew up in an violent home. As a child, John Jr. longed for his father's approval. Instead, the boy got ridicule and contempt from John Sr. The boy grew up determined to prove that he was not as "dumb and stupid" as his dad thought.

John Wayne Gacy in a 1978 photo. Like many serial killers, Gacy grew up in an abusive home.

Not only did John have to contend with his father's alcoholism, but he was also the victim of childhood sexual abuse. When he was four, a fifteen-year-old neighbor girl fondled him. When John was seven, a contractor friend of his father's used to "wrestle" with the boy, locking his head between his legs.

John became determined to show the world that he was somebody. As a teenager, he had a paper route, mowed lawns, and worked as a grocery-delivery boy. In high school his drive to be somebody resulted in his holding offices in school government and volunteering in local political campaigns.

But no matter what young Gacy did, his father always found fault with it. He accused his son of being "softhearted" and "dumb," and Gacy took every word to heart. Deep inside, Gacy believed his father was right. He *was* dumb and stupid.

On His Own

When Gacy was twenty, he left home with the hope that he could be free from his father's disapproval forever, landing eventually in Las Vegas. Once there, Gacy got a job in a mortuary. While he was there, he saw how bodies were embalmed. He was fascinated by the fact that embalmed bodies did not bleed. He wanted to conduct experiments on his own.

After getting a job in a mortuary such as this one, Gacy became fascinated with the embalming process (pictured).

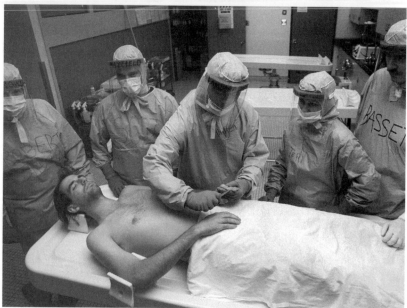

One night, when everyone was gone, Gacy conducted an experiment that haunted him for the rest of his life. Writer Tim Cahill tells the story:

> He was alone and it was dark. The lights were off and it was after midnight, in the secret time, when the dark flower blooms. And there was a coffin, silver-gray, with a white interior. . . . John got inside with the body. He wanted to feel death, in the darkness. And there was a fear, a terrible fear, like someone coming who would discover him there, only there was no sound at all, no one to find him, and he was still afraid.[21]

That night he called his mother and asked to come home.

When he returned home, Gacy graduated from business college and got a job as a shoe salesman. He met and married a coworker named Marlynn, whose parents owned a number of Kentucky Fried Chicken franchises in Iowa. Gacy's new father-in-law offered him a job as manager of one of the restaurants. Gacy took it, and the young Gacy family moved to Iowa.

Soon Gacy had two children, a boy and a girl. He became involved in the Jaycees, an organization of young entrepreneurs, and worked hard as manager. He volunteered in the community. Everyone who knew Gacy thought him to be a hard worker and a devoted family man. Despite his reputation as a good father and husband, some people whispered that he was homosexual. But few people believed the rumors.

What people did not know was that Gacy was leading two lives. Most of the time he was John Gacy, family man and community leader. But Gacy spent some evenings in the seedier side of Waterloo, Iowa, picking up teenage male prostitutes or runaways for sex.

Gacy's First Arrest

One day, Gacy invited a teenaged employee to his home. The boy had no reason to distrust his boss, so he accepted. When they got there, Gacy chatted with the boy, offering him drugs and alcohol. Then, according to the account the boy told later, Gacy tied him up and raped him.

When Gacy was arrested for the attack in the spring of 1968, none of his friends could believe it. However, during the investigation Gacy hired another teenager to attack the boy as retribution for testifying against him. The police soon discovered that Gacy was behind the attack, and that charge added to his problems.

During the investigation, Gacy was ordered to undergo psychiatric evaluation to determine if he was competent to stand trial. One writer comments:

Upon evaluation, Gacy was found to be mentally competent. However, he was considered to be an antisocial personality who would probably not benefit from any known medical treatment. Soon after health authorities submitted the report, Gacy pleaded guilty to the charge of sodomy.[22]

Gacy was sentenced to ten years in prison. As soon as Gacy entered prison, his wife filed for divorce on the grounds that he had violated their marriage vows. The divorce was quickly granted.

In 1968, Gacy was sentenced to ten years in prison for raping a teenage boy. He was released after serving only eighteen months.

The ending of his marriage was followed shortly by another loss. While Gacy was in prison, his father died. His requests to attend his father's funeral were denied. Despite the abuse he had suffered at the hands of his father, Gacy cried like a child because he could not say goodbye.

Even though Gacy seethed with anger and frustration on the inside, he realized that he could get out faster if he behaved himself. To prison authorities, then, he seemed the model prisoner. On June 18, 1970, only eighteen months after he was sent to prison, Gacy was granted parole and released. He decided to start fresh in Chicago.

For a while he worked as a chef. But Gacy continued to cruise the lower-class areas, looking for boys. Sometimes they would go willingly, and Gacy would pay them for sex. Other times, it was different. A few months after Gacy was released from prison, he was arrested again. According to police, Gacy had forced a young boy to have sex with him. Gacy's story, of course, was different. Writer Tim Cahill recounts the story:

What happened, Gacy said, was that he had picked up the kid, who was hitchhiking, and . . . the kid had made a sexual proposition. Gacy said he got so mad that he threw the kid out of the car. . . . John told the docs what made him so mad was that the . . . kid picked him out as someone who'd "get into it." . . . "The cop asked me, 'Couldn't you tell the kid was gay?' Well, no, [Gacy said], because at that time I was trusting and naive."[23]

Luck was with Gacy, however. The boy never showed up to testify against him, so the charges were dropped. Gacy was free to get on with his life.

After he put his legal troubles behind him, the ambitious Gacy soon started his own contracting business. Gacy worked long hours, taking jobs no one else wanted, making a name for himself. However, Gacy always found time to cruise the bus station and local parks. He found plenty of boys willing to have sex with him in exchange for money. During this time he also met a newly divorced mother of two named Carol. She enjoyed the attention Gacy showered on her and they were soon married.

It seemed that Gacy was turning his life around, and by December of 1971, Gacy was released from parole. Appearances were deceptive, however. He would kill his first victim a little over a week later, in January of 1972.

The Killing Begins

Gacy found a boy at the bus station, took him home for sex, and sometime during the night murdered him. He later claimed that this first murder was an accident, that he had killed the boy in self-defense. In any case, Gacy was faced with a dead body for the first time. He opened up a trapdoor in the floor and buried him in the crawl space under the house. Twenty-eight more bodies would join this one in its dank resting place.

For the next three years Gacy was busy. He settled into life with his new wife and her daughters by her previous marriage. His business grew. He worked in political campaigns. He organized parades and celebrations. He was photographed with then–First Lady Rosalynn Carter, a proud moment for the whole family. He hosted huge parties at his home, inviting hundreds of neighbors, friends, and local celebrities. He began appearing at hospitals and events dressed as Pogo the clown.

He was also killing young boys at a steady pace. Writer Michael Newton tells how Gacy went about his grim task:

In searching for prey, Gacy sometimes fell back on young friends and employees, more often trolling the streets of

One of Gacy's self-portraits of Pogo the clown. During the time Gacy was killing boys, he was also appearing at hospitals and civic events dressed as Pogo.

Chicago for hustlers and runaways. . . . He would sometimes flash a badge and gun, "arresting" his intended victim. Others were invited to the Gacy home for drinks, a game of pool, and Gacy would show them "tricks" with "magic handcuffs.". . . When he was finished, Gacy would do the "rope trick"—strangulation.[24]

By this time Gacy had perfected his routine. Pick up a boy, take him home, give him a drink or some food, tie him up or handcuff him, rape him, kill him, then dispose of the body in the crawl space under the house. Years later when he was caught, he would claim to have no memory of most of his victims. He would even suggest that other people killed his victims.

There was one weakness in Gacy's method: the large number of corpses created a terrible smell. Friends and neighbors began complaining of the stench in Gacy's house. Carol kept after Gacy to do something about it, but he never seemed to get around to taking care of the problem. Gradually, Carol began to notice other odd behaviors. Gacy had business meetings in the middle of the night. He yelled at her for the smallest mistakes. He would bring his teenaged employees home at all hours. When he did spend time with Carol, he had no interest at all in sex.

Finally Carol had enough. In 1976 she left Gacy and took the girls with her. At first Gacy was distraught. By that time, though, his fantasy life was taking over. Between April and June of 1976 he killed five boys and buried them in the crawl space. In October of that year he killed two boys in one night and buried them together. Not all of his victims were "low-lifes," as Gacy sometimes called them. Some were simply boys who were in the wrong place at the wrong time. One boy vanished as he was walking home one block from his sister's house. Another boy disappeared while returning from a concert.

The killings continued into 1977 and 1978. Writer Tim Cahill suggests that there was a clear pattern in Gacy's choice of victims:

> Most of the dead boys were of a single physical type. The typical victim was slender, muscular, short. Seventeen of them had been between 5 feet 2 and 5 feet 9, and all had weighed less than 150 pounds. The composite victim was young—twenty of them were under twenty and the youngest

An investigator stands by pictures of faces reconstructed from skulls found in the crawl space of Gacy's house. Most of the boys fit a single physical type.

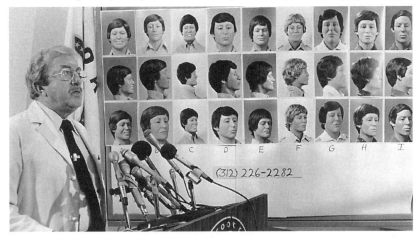

was fourteen; the rest were under twenty-two. The over-whelming majority of them, nineteen of the victims, had light-colored hair; sandy blond, red, or light brown.[25]

Eventually, detectives would discover the correlation among the boys. They all resembled the teenager whose testimony had sent Gacy to prison back in 1968. He had been young, slight, blond, and in Gacy's mind, dangerous. Cahill relates how Gacy saw these youngsters:

> The dumb-looking, dewy-eyed ones, John knew, were the most dangerous. They could use it, the naive act, to out-smart you. Greedy little bastards with "deviate minds." Healthy boys who wore tight-fitting clothes on a small, tightly-muscled frame. Trick minds hiding behind innocent baby faces.[26]

Inexplicably, Gacy let a few of his victims live. One evening in December of 1977, Gacy offered Robert Donnelly a ride. Gacy took him home, raped him, then released him. A few months later Jeff Ringall accepted Gacy's invitation to his house for a drink. Suddenly Gacy grabbed him and chloroformed him. When Jeff awoke, he was tied to a "torture rack," and being raped and beaten. Hours later, Jeff awoke in a nearby park and immediately reported Gacy to police. They began investigating Gacy. But his friends rallied around him, still refusing to believe the outrageous accusations.

By this time Gacy was spinning out of control. In December of 1978, Gacy realized that there was no room left in the crawl space. Gacy threw each of the last four victims in the rushing Des Plaines River. Police later called these victims "floaters." The new disposal method seemed to work well, but Gacy's killing career was about to come crashing to a halt.

Gacy's Last Victim

In the early evening of December 12, 1978, Gacy went to a local drugstore and met Robert Piest, a fifteen-year-old stock boy. As his mother waited for him to get off work, Rob told her he was going out to the parking lot to see a guy named Gacy about a job. Rob never returned. Finally, the family called the police.

Gacy had taken Rob back to his house. Later Gacy claimed that a "fog" kept him from remembering what happened, but he did remember answering the phone. When he returned to the bed-room, he "found" Rob's body on the floor with a rope around his neck. The rope had been twisted tight with a hammer handle, in the manner of a tourniquet. How the scene affected Gacy is retold by Tim Cahill:

> The boy's body was wedged between the bed and the wall. . . . He [John] put the body up on the bed, careful to roll it over on the back because he'd already urinated on his pants. . . . He was disgusted with the kid. Because Rob Piest didn't have to die. . . . Looking at the rope around the boy's neck, he could see that it had been twisted only twice. The hammer handle was turned a bit so that it rested behind the boy's head. Piest could have ducked his head and lowered his shoulder and the hammer handle would have spun loose.[27]

Gacy left Rob's body on his bed, took a shower, and went to a meeting. When he returned, he stashed Rob's body in the attic. The next day he worked a full day and returned home as if nothing had happened. In the meantime, police had discovered Gacy's past conviction and other charges against him. Lieutenant Joseph Kozencyzak of the Des Plaines police decided to pay Gacy a visit.

Lieutenant Kozencyzak and the other officers entered Gacy's house and were overwhelmed by the odd smell. As Lieutenant Kozencyzak sat in Gacy's living room, he had no idea that the boy he was searching for was just a few feet above his head. A few days later Rob's body was found floating in the Des Plaines River.

Gacy's Capture

Convinced that Gacy was hiding something, Lieutenant Kozencyzak got a search warrant for Gacy's home. Officers found quite a few souvenirs of Gacy's crimes, including drivers' licenses and high school class rings; marijuana and rolling papers; a pair of handcuffs with keys; homosexual pornographic books and magazines; police badges; a syringe, needle, and small brown bottle; and nylon rope. In a trash can, they also found a store receipt that they would eventually link to Rob Piest.

Kozencyzak discovered that a number of Gacy's teenaged employees had been reported missing over the years. When questioned, one of Gacy's employees admitted to having had sexual relations with Gacy. Kozencyzak ordered Gacy's house searched again.

At that moment, however, there was insufficient evidence to arrest Gacy for murder, so Kozencyzak decided to have him followed. Twenty-four hours a day, seven days a week, two police officers tailed Gacy. By now Gacy was coming unglued. While officers continued to follow him, Gacy raced around town like a man possessed. He went to see a close friend named Ron Rhode. That conversation is recounted by Tim Cahill:

"I really came to say good-bye to my best friend for the last time," [Gacy] said.

"What the hell are you talking about?" Rhode said.

[Gacy] walked up to Rhode, put his hands on his "best friend's" shoulders and began crying. "Ron," he said. "I've been a bad boy." Gacy was crying like a ten-year-old. ... "I killed thirty people," he said, "give or take a few."[28]

Police remove the remains of a body from Gacy's Chicago home. Twenty-nine bodies were found in the house, along with a variety of souvenirs from the victims.

Gacy (with head in hands) was finally arrested in 1979 after killing thirty-three boys. Nine of the victims were never identified.

While Gacy was confessing to his friend, police were digging in the crawl space. After only a few shovelfuls of dirt were turned, searchers found a human arm. Gacy was immediately arrested. Although police had been aware that there had been a rash of missing boys in the area, until Gacy was captured no one had suspected that they had a serial killer on their hands.

Gacy's arrest became the sensation of Chicago and the world. While in custody, Gacy drew a detailed map of where each body lay buried. All together, twenty-nine bodies were found at 8213 Summerdale. He had dumped four in the Des Plaines River, bringing his grim total to thirty-three. Nine of the victims were never identified.

The Killer Clown Goes to Trial

By the time Gacy's trial began on February 6, 1980, he had been through months of psychiatric evaluation. Gacy insisted that he had no memory of the murders. Gacy told them about Jack, his "alter ego" who came out and killed all those boys whenever Gacy drank or took drugs. One expert on serial murders reports:

> When examined by psychiatrists, Gacy showed no signs of aggression or violence. . . . But his polite, gentle veneer disintegrated when the examiners gave him liquor to drink in an experiment. The change was dramatic. Gacy showed a violent side that perhaps only a few had lived to see.[29]

Gacy blamed Jack for everything and he could not understand why no one else could see that he was not really responsible for any of the murders. He also explained that his victims were beneath contempt, almost not human. He told them that his victims brought their fates on themselves.

> I don't know why I should feel sorry for them. . . . They don't deserve to live, so you don't let them live. . . . You can outsmart somebody and fix him good. They trust you, you can trick 'em into doing anything you want. All you do is, you put the rope around their neck. Tell 'em it's just a trick, there's nothing wrong with it. . . . They put the rope on themselves, they kill themselves.[30]

During the trial, Gacy's lawyers argued that he was insane. The prosecution was determined to prove that Gacy was not only sane, but a truly evil person who should be sentenced to death. Although Gacy allowed his lawyers to portray him as insane, he was determined to avoid that label. Gacy once told Robert Ressler, the famed serial killer expert, that "I thought that [the doctors] were flakes. My personal opinion is that the insanity defense does not belong in the courtroom, not in the legal system at all. I don't even believe it should be used."[31]

Some of the trial testimony was horrifying. One officer testified that Gacy recited the Twenty-third Psalm ["The Lord is my shepherd, I shall not want . . ."] to one of his victims as he strangled him. Gacy had once bragged during a confession that he'd once "done a double," killed two boys at once and buried them together. Family members of the victims took the stand and broke down when shown articles of their sons' clothing and personal items. Gacy hated the families the most. Tim Cahill reports Gacy's reaction to them:

They were sitting together in the courtroom, the families, and Gacy could feel the heat of their hatred burning into his back. If he could just get into a room with all of them for fifteen minutes, he could explain himself, let them see his side of the whole deal. Show them that he was a "scapegoat" and a "victim."[32]

Most psychiatrists agreed that Gacy was a dangerous sociopath. A sociopath may commit horrible crimes, such as rape or murder, but he commits them as a matter of free will and not because of any mental illness. According to the experts who testified at the trial, Gacy knew what he was doing. He killed because he wanted to.

The jury agreed that Gacy should be held responsible for his crimes. On March 12, 1980, John Wayne Gacy was found sane and guilty of murder. A little more than two hours after they reached the verdict, they returned the sentence: death. The courtroom burst into applause.

Fourteen Years on Death Row

The court ordered that Gacy be executed by lethal injection, but it would be fourteen years before the sentence was carried out.

One of Gacy's paintings burns in a bonfire. Family members of Gacy's victims gathered to burn some of his artwork after his execution.

While his lawyers struggled to get his sentence overturned, Gacy settled into prison life. He painted oil pictures of himself made up as Pogo the clown and sold them around the world. He granted interviews and allowed psychiatrists from around the country to evaluate him. Throughout it all, he loudly professed his innocence.

Time finally ran out for Gacy. In May of 1994, he was executed by lethal injection.

CHAPTER 7

Smart and Deadly: Ted Bundy

It was January 1978, but the weather in Tallahassee, Florida, was warm and sunny. The tropical mugginess hung over the low buildings of Florida State University. The local papers had quite a few "For Rent" ads, and a newcomer to town was methodically going through them. Eventually he found a place at a run-down rooming house near campus.

The looks of the room were unimportant. As he signed his lease using the name Chris Hagen, he had to smile. Just a few days before he had been an inmate in Colorado, planning his own defense in a murder trial. He was now an anonymous stranger in a college town far away. As Ted Bundy made his way to his room, he felt a burst of freedom. He could do anything he wanted here. Anything.

Bundy's Early Life

In early 1946, Ted Bundy's mother, Louise Cowell, had been swept off her feet by a dashing military veteran, who disappeared when he discovered that she was pregnant. To keep the illegitimate pregnancy quiet, Louise's family did what many families did at that time: They sent her to a home for unwed mothers. On November 12, 1946, Theodore Cowell was born.

Louise returned home to Philadelphia with her baby and a well-rehearsed story. From now on, Louise would tell the boy that she was his sister, not his mother. Bundy grew up believing that his grandparents were Mom and Dad. Although today there is some dispute whether Bundy knew that his "sister" was really his mother, Bundy himself said that he did not learn the truth until years later.

When Bundy was four, he and Louise moved to Tacoma, Washington. Soon Louise married Johnnie Bundy. A few years later they had a daughter, Linda, and over the next few years, three other children were added to the Bundy family: Glen, Sandra, and

Richard. Ted eventually took Bundy's name as his own.

By all accounts, Ted's early years were normal. His mother, whom he still thought was his sister, and Johnnie loved Ted and treated him as they did the rest of their children. Louise recognized Ted's intelligence and urged him to do well in school. Ted even had a dog, a collie he named Lassie.

Although the Bundy family was comfortable, they were not rich. Ted was ashamed of the cars that Johnnie drove and of the modest houses they lived in. To get the things he thought he deserved, Ted began stealing. In high school Bundy was charged with auto theft and burglary, but because he was a juvenile, records of the crimes were sealed when he turned eighteen.

Embarrassed by his family's modest lifestyle, Ted Bundy began to steal the things he thought he deserved. While still in high school, he was charged with auto theft and burglary.

Then there was Ted's unpredictable temper. Even in elementary school, the boy would fly into uncontrollable rages. One of his childhood friends noted:

> It was really easy to see when Ted got mad. His eyes turned just about black. . . . He has blue eyes that are kind of flecked with darker colors. When he gets hot, they seem to get less blue and more dark. . . . Someone would just say something, and you could just see it in his face. The dark flecks seemed to expand.[33]

However, most people noticed no odd emotional problems with Ted. He made good grades in school and joined numerous clubs and activities. He always felt out of place, however, because of his small size and his looks. He only had one date in high school because he felt so insecure about his appearance.

He also had no idea how people formed relationships, nor had he any idea how to care for others or empathize with another person. Writers Michaud and Aynesworth write that, for Bundy, responding to others was all part of an elaborate charade:

Bundy's critical challenge from his teen years onward was the perfection and maintenance of a credible public persona, his mask of sanity. Lacking true adult emotions, he had to put on the look of normalcy while inside the tumult raged unabated. . . . It was painful and confusing to him, each frequent misstep a stab at the child bewildered by his inability to handle the simplest adult relationships.[34]

Bundy's College Years

Bundy's grades were good enough to earn him a scholarship to the University of Puget Sound in Washington. But Bundy's first year in college was a failure. The usually gregarious Bundy lived at home, which kept him from making friends and feeling like a part of college life. His grades were terrible and he seemed unable to focus on anything. The one bright moment that year came when Bundy purchased his very first car: a 1968 Volkswagen. Bundy loved VW bugs and one would eventually become famous as the car Bundy used to kidnap his victims.

In his sophomore year Bundy transferred to the University of Washington and changed his major to Chinese studies—a glamorous, unusual major that won him the attention that he so desperately craved. Bundy immersed himself in school. He made friends, his grades shot up, and he finally felt as though his life were on track. This was also the year he met Stephanie.

Stephanie was smart, beautiful, and from a wealthy California family. Bundy could not believe that someone with her class would

By majoring in Chinese studies at the University of Washington, Bundy finally got the attention he craved.

want him. Bundy fell madly in love. Gradually, however, Stephanie realized that Bundy had no ambition or direction in his life. After a year, she broke off their relationship.

Bundy was devastated by the breakup. He dropped out of school and traveled the country, numb and confused. Eventually, in the fall of 1969, he returned to Washington. One night, at a club with friends, he met Meg, a recently divorced young mother with a small daughter. A few months later they moved in together.

Bundy's life again seemed on an upswing. He enrolled in school again, this time as a psychology major. He volunteered as a counselor in a crisis clinic, answering calls from distraught people who were contemplating suicide.

But Bundy also had a darker side. Continuing a practice from years past, he broke into houses, stealing the objects he needed to maintain his lifestyle. No one in Bundy's life had any idea of what he was doing, mainly because he was so good at acting. As he later admitted:

> I'm capable of being genuinely cheerful and gregarious—at least for a limited period of time. . . . I became expert at projecting something very different. That I was very busy, I had a huge part of my life that nobody knew about. It didn't take much effort at all.[35]

In the spring of 1972 Bundy graduated with a degree in psychology. He decided to try law school and was eventually accepted into the University of Puget Sound law school for the fall 1973 term. About the time he began law school, he met up with Stephanie. She was astounded that her former boyfriend had gone from an immature young man to a stylish, self-confident law student. For a few months they met secretly, and soon Bundy proposed marriage. Then without warning, he told Stephanie never to call him again. His plan all along had been to reject her as she had rejected him. He wanted her to feel the same pain that she had inflicted on him.

Bundy had succeeded in his plan of revenge, but he was failing law school and sliding into another depression. On the outside, he was still the charming, gregarious Bundy. Inside, though, the monster was taking over.

Bundy Begins Killing

Although it was never proven conclusively, it is believed that Bundy's first victim was a teenage runaway named Kathy Devine. In the fall of 1973 she had decided to hitchhike from Washington to Oregon. When her body was discovered in Washington on December 6, she had been strangled, sodomized, and her throat had been cut.

Two subsequent disappearances were later attributed to Bundy, although he was not a suspect at the time. On January 31, 1974, Lynda Healey disappeared from her basement apartment in Seattle. Police found her mattress covered with blood and a nightgown with blood on the collar. On March 12, 1974, Donna Manson, a student at Evergreen State College in Olympia, Washington, went to a jazz concert and was never seen again.

The police were unaware at first that the crimes were linked. But there were a few similarities. For one thing, the victims looked alike: pretty young women who parted their long hair in the middle. Once the disappearances had made the news, other women began telling stories about odd encounters with an attractive man wearing a cast on one hand. Ann Rule, a friend of Bundy's from his early years writes of one of these incidents:

> One girl said she'd talked to a tall, handsome man in his twenties . . . who had one arm in a sling and a metal brace on his finger. He had trouble managing his armload of books and had dropped several. "Finally, he asked me if I'd help him carry them to his car," she said . . . the car, a Volkswagen bug, was parked nearby. She'd carried his books to the car, and then noticed the passenger seat was missing. Something caused the hairs on the back of her neck to stand on end, something about the missing seat. . . . Suddenly she just wanted to be away from him.[36]

She dropped his books and ran. Others were less fortunate.

On July 14, 1974, Bundy made his way to Lake Sammanish, a popular park. The area was overflowing with people. He lingered beside the cinder block ladies' bathroom and chatted with women who walked past. When Janice Ott approached the restroom, Bundy introduced himself and asked for help loading a sailboat into his car. She agreed and innocently got into his car.

He drove her to an isolated cabin a few miles from the lake. There he tied her up, assaulted her, then returned to the park. A few hours later, Bundy approached Denise Naslund, who agreed to help him. He drove her to the same cabin where Janice was still imprisoned, pulled a knife, and forced her inside.

Later Bundy would imply that he assaulted one girl while the other watched, then killed them both. Only Bundy knew for sure. By that afternoon, however, Janice and Denise's friends and families were frantic. The women, like the others, had vanished. The police had a big clue, however. Other women remembered a friendly guy named "Ted" who had asked them for help. Police now had a name and a description. The hunt was on.

At the end of the summer, Bundy left Washington, having transferred to law school in Utah. Not long after the semester started, reports of missing women in Utah began surfacing. Melissa Smith left home to go to a slumber party and was never seen again. Nine days later her body was discovered east of Salt Lake City. She had been raped, strangled, and beaten with a crowbar. Strangely, her hair had been freshly shampooed and her nails done, as if the killer had taken care of her body before he dumped it.

On Halloween, 1974, Laura Aime disappeared. Her body would not be found for almost a month, beaten beyond recognition. On November 8, Carol DeRonch was walking in the Fashion Place Mall in Murray, Utah, when a man introduced himself as "Officer Roseland" and explained that he needed her in the mall security office. She got in his car, a beat-up VW bug. But instead of going to an office, Bundy pulled over and tried to handcuff Carol. Carol managed to escape, and she went straight to the police.

The 1968 Volkswagen bug that belonged to Ted Bundy. Bundy used the car to kidnap a number of his victims.

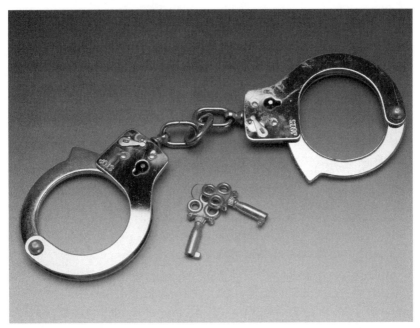

Bundy used handcuffs to immobilize his victims, who were usually attractive young women who parted their hair in the middle.

Enraged at this failure, Bundy drove twenty miles north to Bountiful, Utah. He stopped at a high school and slipped into the auditorium as the audience watched a school play. Bundy spoke to people backstage. Later, he was nowhere to be found. Neither was Debbie Kent, a student who had gone to her car during intermission. Witnesses later reported that they had seen a VW bug speeding away from the school. The police found a small handcuff key in the parking lot. The key fit the handcuffs Carol DeRonch was wearing when she escaped. Then the Utah disappearances suddenly halted.

A Move to Colorado

Before long, however, women began to be reported missing in Colorado ski country. In January of 1975, Caryn Campbell disappeared from a resort hotel hallway. In March, ski instructor Julie Campbell disappeared, never to be found. Denise Oliverson disappeared in April and was never found.

By this time, police in three states were beginning to realize that the same man might be responsible for many of the murders. Officers compared notes, made composite sketches, and talked to dozens of witnesses. Police needed a big break. They got it on August 16, 1975.

Bundy Is Captured for the First Time

In the early hours of that hot August night, Officer Bob Hayward of the Utah Highway Patrol noticed an unfamiliar VW driving slowly through his neighborhood. He shone his lights on the license plate, and to his surprise the car sped away. After a brief chase, the VW pulled into a gas station. The driver, Ted Bundy, was wearing dark clothing. He told Officer Hayward that he'd just been to see a movie but gotten lost. To Officer Hayward, the man's story sounded suspicious. He later told of the incident:

> I looked in the front seat and there was not a seat on the passenger side . . . deputies looked in the car and . . . came up with a few other items of interest that a person coming from a movie normally would not carry such as an ice pick, a pair of handcuffs, silk stockings with holes cut in for the eyes and nose, and other items that a burglar might carry. . . . We impounded the car and I took Mr. Bundy to the County Jail and booked him on the charge of "Attempting to Evade a Police Officer."[37]

Some of the other items found in Bundy's car included a flashlight, gloves, strips of torn sheeting, and a knit ski mask. Bundy was arrested for possession of burglary tools. One officer, Detective Jerry Thompson, suspected that Ted Bundy might be the murderous "Ted" that police had been seeking for so long. When he showed Bundy's picture to witnesses, including Carol DeRonch, they identified him.

But the police needed more evidence. By October, they had gathered enough evidence to put Bundy in a lineup. He was confident that he would be set free, but all the witnesses identified him. Bundy was arrested for the kidnapping and attempted murder of Carol DeRonch. On Monday, March 1, 1976, Ted Bundy was convicted of kidnapping and sentenced to one to fifteen years in prison.

Bundy Escapes

As Bundy adjusted to life in prison, detectives in three states continued digging for clues. The more that Colorado detectives looked into Bundy's history, the more they were convinced that he was responsible for dozens of murders.

For months they pieced together evidence, and finally had enough to charge him with the murder of Caryn Campbell. Bundy was transferred to a jail in Colorado to await trial. But

Carol DeRonch testifies at a pre-sentencing hearing for Bundy. He was convicted of kidnapping DeRonch from a suburban Salt Lake City shopping mall in 1974.

Bundy was not inclined to take his chances with a jury. One day, when he was allowed to visit the courthouse law library, Bundy jumped from a second-story window and ran away. He fled to the nearby mountains as police set up roadblocks and began searching the area. A few days later Bundy was caught trying to leave town in a stolen car.

Back in prison, Bundy managed to convince the judge to let him serve as his own attorney. He was given a phone in his cell and time in the law library to work on his defense. All the time, he was forming a new plan. For eight weeks, every night when the prison was quiet and the guards were elsewhere, Bundy used a stolen hacksaw to cut a twelve inch by twelve inch square in the ceiling of his cell. Then on December 30, 1977, he decided it was time to make his move. Writer Michael Cartel picks up the story:

> He told the jailer that he wouldn't want breakfast, then stuffed papers under his blanket and squeezed into the ceiling. He found an opening that led to a prison employee's home closet, changed into the civilian clothes that

just happened to be there, and walked out the front door. A car was sitting outside with the keys conveniently left in the ignition and Ted Bundy was gone. . . . Fifteen hours later the jailer, bringing lunch, discovered legal papers and law books instead of Ted under the covers.[38]

Bundy took a bus to Denver, then flew on to Chicago, where he stole another car. Then Bundy set out for Florida.

Freedom in Florida

Once he arrived in Tallahassee, Bundy assumed the identity of a former Florida State student, Chris Hagen. He stole enough objects to furnish a modest room. But Bundy's mind was spiraling downward quickly. The stress of the escape, combined with the problems of finding a place to live, and the legions of pretty young women on campus were overwhelming. His urge to kill began taking over.

Late on the evening of January 14, 1978, Bundy discovered an open back door into the Chi Omega sorority house. Beside the house was a pile of firewood, so Bundy picked up a short log and wrapped it in cloth. Then he crept upstairs.

The house was full of young women, some sleeping, some up late talking with one another in their rooms. One student, Nita Neary, had just come home from a date when she heard a *thud* from upstairs. Reporters Stephen Michaud and Hugh Aynesworth relate what she saw next:

> Standing in the foyer about sixteen feet from the sorority's tall double front doors, she heard the footfalls coming down the carpeted staircase to her left. Then she saw the man; he was crouched low by the front doors. His left hand was on the door handle. In his right hand, which was nearer her, she could see what looked like a club, wrapped in some sort of dark material. He was wearing a dark knit cap, pulled low, almost to his eyebrows.[39]

The man disappeared through the door. Nita's first thought was that the house had been burglarized. But when Nita went upstairs, she saw her friend Karen Chandler stumbling in the hallway, blood streaming down her face. The attacker had viciously broken her jaw and fractured her skull. Karen's roommate, Kathy Kleiner, was found moaning on her bed, blood everywhere.

Soon police and ambulances poured onto the scene. While paramedics tended to the injured girls, police grimly searched the rest of the rooms. In one they found the body of Lisa Levy. She had been strangled, violently bitten, and sexually assaulted. In another room they found Margaret Bowman, who had been strangled and hit on the head with such force that her skull had been crushed.

Bundy was not finished that night, however. While police were still at the Chi Omega house, he broke into twenty-one-year-old Cheryl Thomas's apartment eight blocks away and attacked the sleeping girl. Police found her bleeding and semiconscious.

Bundy Is Caught

Ted Bundy was now completely out of control. Like many serial killers, Bundy had given himself over completely to his violent fantasies. Writers Michaud and Aynesworth explain what was happening to Bundy: "One mark of these final days was his total recklessness; Bundy acted as if nothing could touch him. He also regressed, behaving more and more like a child and abandoning the mask of sanity. . . . He and the 'entity' had fused."[40]

A few days after the Chi Omega murders, Bundy stole a white Dodge van and headed for Jacksonville, Florida. His first intended

Upon his arrival in Tallahassee, Bundy settled in the vicinity of Florida State University. Bundy killed two female students and wounded three others in the area surrounding the university.

victim was a fourteen-year-old girl named Leslie Parmenter. Bundy approached her as she waited for a ride home and began asking her questions. Fortunately, her brother appeared and, suspicious of a stranger talking to his sister, confronted him. Bundy headed toward Lake City, Florida. Bundy then spied twelve-year-old Kimberly Leach walking to class at Lake City Junior High. Her body would be discovered eight weeks later in a state park.

Bundy raced back to Tallahassee where he dumped the van, stole an orange VW bug, and loaded up his belongings. Now disoriented and panic-stricken, Bundy headed to Pensacola. There, a police officer spotted the VW in an unfamiliar area. As before, Bundy fled, and the officer gave chase. Finally the officer stopped the car and arrested him.

Bundy Goes to Trial

As Bundy sat in a Florida prison, investigators found evidence in the van and on Kimberly's clothing that linked Bundy to her murder. On July 31, 1978, Bundy was charged with the murder of Kimberly Leach. Soon after, he was charged with the Chi Omega murders as well.

The first trial, for the Chi Omega murders, was a media circus. The most damaging evidence against Bundy was the bite mark left on Lisa Levy's body. It was proven that the bite mark came from Ted Bundy. That testimony, as well as the recollections of the witnesses, sealed Bundy's fate. He was found guilty of murder and sentenced to die in the electric chair. Bundy still refused to accept responsibility for his crimes or their consequences. Observers wrote: "Inside him, a guilty verdict could be ignored as meaningless, and furthermore he could rationalize the expected decision as a terrible mistake, the fault of someone else. The blame, he decided, would go to his attorneys."[44]

His trial for the murder of Kimberly Leach was no less sensational. During the trial Bundy yelled from his seat and disrupted proceedings. He would scream "Liar! Liar!" to the witnesses as they testified. Bundy's theatrics did no good. On February 7, 1980, Bundy was convicted of the murder of Kimberly Leach.

Unrepentant to the End

Throughout the rest of his life, Bundy would never take responsibility for any of his crimes. The only way Bundy would discuss the crimes was as if he were "speculating" about how a murder "might" have been committed. Years later, his last attorney, Polly Nelson, would recall a discussion she had with Bundy about Kimberly Leach's murder:

"Ted, I saw a file of statements from people who claimed to have seen Kimberly Leach some time after she'd disappeared from school."

Ted said nothing, but grew still. . . . This was the first time I was talking to him as the perpetrator of the crimes, not just as a trial participant, but I still didn't dare to be direct.

"Ted," I finally asked, "is there any possibility that any of the reports could have been true?"

Ted waited another minute more, then shook his head. This was his first direct admission of guilt.[42]

During his trial for the murder of Kimberly Leach, Bundy would scream at witnesses as they testified. His performance failed to prevent him from being convicted of the murder.

On the day of Bundy's execution, a man hawks shirts outside of the Florida State Prison. The carnival-like atmosphere was indicative of the hatred people felt toward Bundy.

Execution Day

For nine years Bundy was on death row in Florida. Time after time, his lawyers tried and failed, to get his convictions overturned. The entire time, he was convinced that he would somehow be immune to his fate. But on January 24, 1989, Ted Bundy was proven wrong and was executed in Florida's electric chair.

Outside the prison on execution day, throngs of people celebrated, waving signs that read "Fry-Day" and "Ted Bundy Dies." The carnival-like atmosphere outside hinted at the pure hatred and horror that Ted Bundy instilled in the American people. Even today, his name is synonymous with the term "serial killer."

CHAPTER 8

Mild-Mannered Monster: Jeffrey Dahmer

In downtown Milwaukee, Wisconsin, the homeless push squeaky shopping carts piled with lumpy garbage bags through grimy neighborhoods. Drug dealers take over abandoned buildings and prostitutes work the streets. In these neighborhoods, most people keep to themselves. It's not easy—or safe—to get to know the neighbors.

Few noticed a quiet, blond man who lived in the neighborhood. Those that did paid little attention. They never noticed all the boys and men who visited the man known as "Jeff." No one noticed that many who entered his apartment did not come out again.

Dahmer's Early Years

Jeffrey Dahmer was born in Milwaukee on May 21, 1960. His parents, Lionel and Joyce Dahmer, were overjoyed. For the first six years of his life Jeff seemed completely normal in every way.

His parents' marriage, however, was a rocky one. Jeffrey's parents fought constantly, and Lionel spent a great deal of time away from the tension of his home life. When Jeffrey was six, the Dahmer family moved to a modest home in Bath, Ohio. Other changes that year made the turmoil in Jeffrey's life more pronounced. Not only was he uprooted from his home, but he began first grade, and his mother gave birth to his younger brother.

According to one observer, little Jeffrey had changed, and not for the better:

> A strange fear had begun to creep into his personality, a dread of others that was combined with a general lack of self-confidence. . . . The little boy who'd once seemed so happy and self-assured had been replaced by a different person, now deeply shy, distant, nearly uncommunicative.[43]

Jeffrey Dahmer sits in the courtroom, facing murder charges.

Unknown to everyone around him, Jeffrey was beginning to have some unusual interests. When Dahmer was in elementary school, Lionel, a chemist, gave his son a basic chemistry set. Dahmer immediately began to figure out how it worked.

> Jeffrey . . . experimented with the chemicals, quickly learning what they could do to insects and small animals. Neighbors recalled Jeffrey's fascination with dead animals, at first merely a child's collection of insects preserved in jars with some type of chemical, but later a stash of dead animals retrieved after they had been run over or hit on the neighboring roadsides.[44]

As a teenager, Dahmer would cruise the streets and freeways, looking for roadkill. He would bring home garbage bags filled with what he'd found on the roadside. Years later, Dahmer described one such outing. "One of them was a large dog found [on] the side of the road, and I was going to strip the flesh off, bleach the bones, and reconstruct it, and sell it. But I never got that far with it. I don't know what started me on this; it's a strange thing to be interested in."[45]

On the other hand, in some ways Jeffrey was quite normal. In high school, Dahmer played clarinet in the band, worked on the school newspaper, and played on the tennis team. He was also known as the class clown. He became so well-known in his high school for horsing around that playing wild jokes became known as "doing a Dahmer."

But the demons had already grasped Dahmer. He had begun drinking and would sit in class sipping alcohol out of a paper cup. Moreover, Dahmer's home life was deteriorating. By the time he was a senior in high school, his parents were in the middle of a bitter divorce. Dahmer was also beginning to realize that he was gay and began to have fantasies that included having sex with male hitchhikers.

Dahmer's sexual frustration, his inability to connect with others, his turbulent home life, and his ever-growing fantasy life finally pushed him over the edge. In June of 1978, Dahmer graduated from high school and killed for the first time.

Dahmer's First Murder

It was summer, and Dahmer's mother and brother had moved out of the house and his father was frequently out of town. The eighteen-year-old boy was left alone in the house to fend for himself. He was lonely and he wanted company. When he saw Steven Hicks, also eighteen, thumb-

During his teenage years, Dahmer was fascinated with dead animals and began bringing home bags filled with roadkill.

ing a ride one evening, it seemed as if Dahmer's dreams were about to come true. Like most serial killers, Dahmer had crossed the line between fantasy and reality. Later he recalled the night to Robert Ressler, an expert on serial killers:

> I was driving back home after drinking, and I wasn't looking for anyone—but about a mile away from the house,

there he was! Hitchhiking along the road. He was attractive. I stopped. . . . And I asked him if he wanted to go back and smoke pot, and he said, "Oh yeah." And we went into my bedroom, had some beer, and from the time I spent with him I could tell he wasn't gay. I didn't know how else to keep him there other than to get the barbell and to hit him over the head, which I did, then strangled him with the same barbell.[46]

After Steven was dead, Dahmer discovered that he was aroused by the idea that he finally had control over someone who would never leave him. He dragged Steven's body to the crawl space under the house and dismembered it with a large hunting knife. Dahmer also discovered that the sight of the internal organs excited him sexually.

That night Dahmer put all the body parts in large garbage bags, threw them in the back seat of his car, and set out to dump the pieces in a ravine. On the way, he was stopped by police. This would be the first time—but not the last—Dahmer was almost caught. Dahmer later told Ressler:

I'm on a deserted country road and I get pulled over by the police for driving left of center. . . . They do the drunk test. I pass that. Shine the flashlight in the backseat, see the bags, ask me what it is. I tell 'em it's garbage I hadn't gotten around to dropping off at the landfill. And they believe it, even though there's a smell. So they give me a ticket for driving left of center and I go back home.[47]

Once Dahmer was home, he buried the body in a drainpipe in the yard. The body would lie there for more than two years. Dahmer's more violent urges would also lie hidden for many years.

Dahmer's Early Adulthood

In January 1979 Dahmer enlisted in the army, having begun and dropped out of college. In the army, Dahmer kept to himself and drank most of the time. Just months before his three-year enlistment time was over, Dahmer was discharged for alcohol and drug abuse.

Upon his return to civilian life, Dahmer moved first to Miami, Florida. After a year, he finally returned to live with his father and stepmother in Bath. One of his first acts was to dig up Steven's body, break his bones apart with a sledgehammer, and scatter the remains.

Members of the sheriff's department search the grounds of Dahmer's former home in Bath, Ohio. Dahmer buried his first victim, Steven Hicks, in a drainpipe in the yard.

Dahmer's behavior grew increasingly worrisome to his family. He would roam the bars, arguing with anyone who wouldn't serve him a drink. He got into fights. Finally, his father sent Dahmer to live with his grandmother in West Allis, Wisconsin.

The Killing Begins in Earnest

For a time, it seemed that Dahmer was thriving in Wisconsin. He and his grandmother, Catherine, were very close. He eventually landed a job at the Ambrosia Chocolate factory and was assigned to the third shift. Reporter Anne Schwartz writes: "Four years went by and on the surface, all seemed calm. . . . He and his grandmother shared a caring relationship, and her neighbors recalled seeing him at work in the yard and helping her with errands."[48]

Until this time, Dahmer was in his cooling-off period, remorseful about the first death and determined not to let it happen again. But Dahmer's fantasy world was slowly consuming him. As his need to control other people grew stronger, he tried to suppress it. He began to realize that his ultimate fantasy was to completely control another person both physically and sexually. But at this point, he still had some hold on reality. He realized that giving in to his fantasies would mean killing. To keep from hurting others, he tried using a mannequin for sex, thinking that if he used a fake body he could satisfy his urges. Soon that wasn't enough.

His next step was to find live partners. He started frequenting the gay bathhouses in Milwaukee, looking for sexual partners. When Dahmer would find a partner at the bathhouse, he would spike the man's drink with sleeping pills and have sex with him while he was unconscious. Later, he confided that he used "the drink" so that he would not have to kill his partners. Eventually he was caught when at one bathhouse the man who drank Dahmer's mixture had to be taken to the hospital. Dahmer was kicked out of the club for good.

Dahmer returned to the gay bars. It had been nine years since the first murder, and Dahmer had tried everything he could think of to get sexual gratification without hurting anyone. But his need for control was overwhelming him.

In the fall of 1987, Dahmer met Steve Toumi at Club 219, a gay bar. They went to a hotel room and Dahmer gave him "the drink." Later Dahmer described what happened.

I remember nothing before waking up in the morning. [Toumi] was on his back, his head was over the edge of the bed, and my forearms were bruised, and he had broken ribs and everything. Apparently I'd beaten him to death. . . . I had to do something with the body. . . . [I bought] a large suitcase, put him in that . . . I check out, get a taxi, have the guy help me put the bag in the back, ride to Grandma's. I take the suitcase, put it in the fruit cellar, and leave it there for about a week.[49]

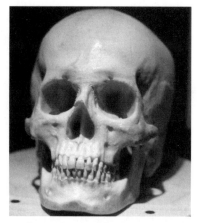

Later Dahmer dismembered the body, stuffed it in a bag, smashed it with a sledgehammer, then threw it in the trash. He tried unsuccessfully to preserve the skull—one of his first trophies—but he finally threw it out, too.

Two months later Dahmer picked up fourteen-year-old Jamie Doxtator and took the boy back to Grandma's house.

Dahmer learned how to preserve the skulls of his victims, which he kept as trophies.

There, he gave the boy "the drink" and, when he passed out, strangled him. He dismembered the body, bagged it, and threw it out. In the next few months he killed Richard Guerrero, bringing his total to four victims.

But by now his grandmother had grown tired of the noise and the young men Dahmer seemed to always have in his basement room. Dahmer and his grandmother decided the best thing would be for him to move out, and that fall he moved into his own apartment, in the downtown area of Milwaukee.

Dahmer Is Arrested

The day after he moved into his new home, Dahmer convinced a thirteen-year-old Laotian boy to pose for nude photos, then gave him "the drink." Dahmer thought the boy was unconscious, but somehow he got away. The next day, Dahmer was arrested for sexual exploitation of a child. The police made a cursory search of Dahmer's apartment and found traces of the drug in a cup. What they failed to find was a skull, buried under clothes in a drawer.

Dahmer pled guilty to the charges and was released on bail. On March 25, 1989, he met Anthony Sears. Dahmer's routine worked again: offering money for photos, taking the man home, giving his victim "the drink," strangling him, dismembering the corpse, and bagging it.

But this time Jeffrey added a new step to the process. Journalist Anne Schwartz describes the addition: "He kept the head and boiled it to remove the skin, later painting it gray, so that in case of discovery, the skull would look like a plastic model used by medical students. Dahmer saved the trophy for two years."[50]

At Dahmer's sentencing on the sexual exploitation charge, prosecutors argued for giving Dahmer five to six years in prison. They stated that they were convinced that Dahmer would reoffend. Dahmer begged the judge to let him have a chance to turn his life around. The judge agreed to give Dahmer a chance. After ten months in a work-release program, Dahmer was granted early release. On May 4, 1990, Dahmer found another apartment and moved into 924 North 25th, apartment 213. For the next year and a half Dahmer would bring a dozen men and boys to his own private slaughterhouse.

Killing Frenzy

By the time Dahmer settled into his new home, he had perfected his routine. Once his victim was dead, however, Dahmer varied his style, depending on his whim. He might first take pictures of the body. Other times he would wait until rigor mortis had set in so that he could pose the body for pictures. He would keep some body parts as trophies. Occasionally he would boil the head in a household cleaner called Soilex to remove the flesh, then spray paint the skull gray.

Dahmer did all this in the name of control. By keeping his partners around him always, Dahmer knew they'd never leave. One victim almost got away, and that incident marked the beginning of the end to Dahmer's reign of terror.

On May 27, 1991, a month before Dahmer's house of carnage was discovered, police were called to

Dahmer killed a dozen men in his apartment in downtown Milwaukee. He was finally arrested on July 22, 1991.

his neighborhood by a report of a young boy, naked, wandering the streets in a daze. A few hours before, fourteen-year-old Konerak Sinthasomphone had agreed to pose for pictures. Dahmer gave him "the drink," then left the unconscious boy while he went for more beer. While Dahmer was gone, Konerak revived and fled.

By the time the officers got to the scene, the boy appeared drunk and disoriented. Dahmer calmly explained that the boy was his nineteen-year-old homosexual lover. He took the officers back to his apartment and showed them his photo ID and the pictures he'd taken of Konerak. Meanwhile, the boy sat quietly on the sofa.

Everything seemed fine to the officers, although they did notice a smell. They did not bother to search the apartment because they had no reason to believe Dahmer was lying to them. Had they looked in the bedroom, however, they would have found a corpse spread out on the bed. After talking to Dahmer for a few minutes more, the officers left. As soon as the officers left, Dahmer strangled Konerak, took photos, severed his head, and disposed of the body.

Dahmer's world was falling apart. By now, Dahmer's fantasies had completely crowded out reality. In three weeks Dahmer killed four more men. Soon after the fourth murder, Dahmer was fired from his job at the chocolate factory. He started drinking steadily and stopped bathing. He received an eviction notice.

Dahmer's Arrest

On July 22, 1991, Dahmer went to a local mall and approached Tracy Edwards, a thirty-two-year-old black man. Edwards agreed to go back to Dahmer's apartment with him. Some time later, Edwards, with handcuffs dangling from one wrist, approached two police officers, Rolf Mueller and Robert Rauth, who were patrolling in Dahmer's neighborhood. He said that some "weird dude" had pulled a knife and had tried to handcuff him. The officers decided to check out Edwards's story.

Dahmer answered the door, invited the officers in, and confirmed that Edwards had been with him. He offered to get the key to the handcuffs from the bedroom. Later, detectives expressed amazement at the calm that Dahmer showed. Robert Ressler notes:

> When Dahmer's last victim escaped his apartment in the midst of being attacked, Dahmer calmly waited for the police to arrive and made no effort to destroy or conceal the great amount of evidence that he kept in his rooms. . . . In the months prior to his arrest Dahmer let outsiders . . . into his apartment when the paraphernalia were present and in full view. . . . All the signs of the killer were there, but no one heeded them.[51]

One of the officers went into Dahmer's bedroom. He noticed Polaroid pictures and took a closer look. Then he realized they were photos of dismembered bodies and skulls. He yelled to his partner to place Dahmer under arrest.

As detectives searched Dahmer's apartment, horror upon horror was revealed. In a lift-top freezer they found human heads in plastic bags. In the back of the bedroom closet was a large stockpot that held decomposing body parts. There were two heads in a computer box and skulls and bones stored in a filing cabinet. In Dahmer's bedroom, detectives found a photo album filled with pictures of corpses.

The bedroom also held the most horrifying object officers recovered. Writer Anne Schwartz says: "In the corner of the bedroom sat an ominous, blue, fifty-seven gallon barrel with a black

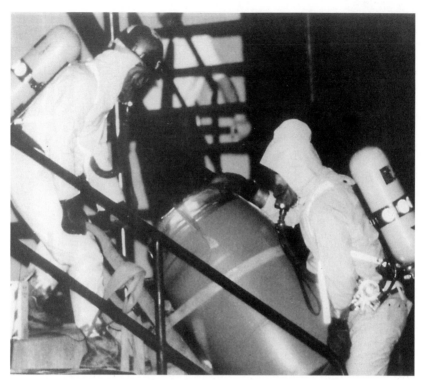

Two men in protective suits remove a barrel from Dahmer's apartment, which contained parts of eleven different bodies soaking in a chemical bath.

lid holding decomposing body parts in a sludgy chemical bath. . . . In all, seven skulls and four heads with flesh still on them were recovered from the apartment."[52]

Dahmer went meekly with the officers. That night he sat in an interrogation room and readily confessed to murder after murder, including the first one when he was eighteen. As officers listened in growing horror, Dahmer described the killings in detail. Anne Schwartz replays the scene:

> As he spoke, Dahmer smoked numerous cigarettes. . . . The room was enveloped in a smoky haze as Dahmer recounted seventeen murders, providing minute details of the crimes. . . . As easily as he talked about his childhood and being an atheist, he talked about being a murderer and a cannibal.[53]

Dahmer's victims were predominantly minorities, and Dahmer explained that this was because he lived in an ethnic neighborhood and those were the men he met. Most of them were adults with long histories of absence from home, which explained why no missing person's reports had ever been filed. Dahmer also said that he would rather not have killed anyone at all. But his overwhelming fear of being alone made him believe that it was better to have his partners dead than to have them leave him.

Sensational Trial

Dahmer's pretrial hearing on January 13, 1992, had the feel of a celebrity event. Anyone who entered the courtroom was searched. To protect Dahmer, a $15,000, eight-foot-high wall of bullet-resistant glass and steel was built around the area where Dahmer would sit. At the hearing, Dahmer pled guilty, saving his lawyers the difficulty of having to prove Dahmer innocent. Their job remained to prove that Dahmer was insane.

The trial to determine Dahmer's sanity began on January 27, 1992. Inside the courtroom, the jury was hearing details of Dahmer's crimes that were beyond comprehension. Gerald Boyle, Dahmer's defense attorney, argued that Dahmer had a craving for sex with dead bodies, combined with a fear of loneliness that grew into a reign of killing that was out of control. Boyle even compared Dahmer to Satan.

Dahmer pleaded guilty to the murders during a pre-trial hearing, but stood trial to determine whether he was insane at the time of the killings. The jury found him guilty and sane.

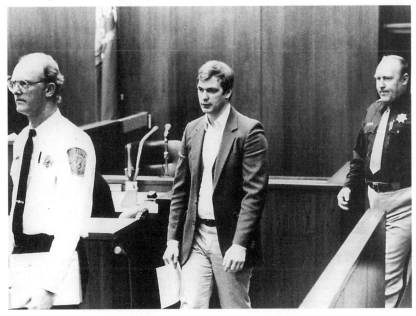

Detail after gory detail emerged: Dahmer's early fascination with dead animals, his obsession with killing and internal organs, his gruesome sexual appetites, the experiments he attempted on his victims, and most importantly, his cannibalism. "He ate the body parts of people because he believed they would come alive in him. . . . [Dahmer] experimented with different types of kitchen seasonings to make the cooked human flesh taste better."[54]

The prosecution was just as determined to prove that Dahmer was not insane but evil. The prosecutor, Mike McCann, painted a picture of Dahmer as a self-absorbed man who killed to satisfy his bizarre sexual cravings. He said that Dahmer's ability to remain calm under pressure showed that he was in control of his actions and understood the consequences.

McCann read parts of Dahmer's confession that stated that Dahmer felt a sense of loss when he killed his victims, but that he also felt excitement. Dahmer confessed that having the victim's bodies in his house made him feel evil.

It took the jury only five hours to return a verdict of guilty and sane. He was sentenced to 957 years in prison. Before he was sentenced, Dahmer read a four-page apology. It read, in part:

> It is now over. This has never been a case of trying to get free. I didn't ever want freedom. Frankly, I wanted death for myself. . . . I hated no one. I knew I was sick or evil or both. . . . I know how much harm I have caused. . . . No matter what I did I could not undo the terrible harm I have caused. My attempt to help identify the remains was the best I could do, and that was hardly anything . . . . Your Honor, I know that you are about to sentence me. I ask for no consideration. . . . I know my time in prison will be terrible, but I deserve whatever I get because of what I have done.[55]

Dahmer's Death in Prison

For two years Dahmer was incarcerated in the Columbia Correctional Institute in Portage, Wisconsin. Although he was treated like every other inmate, precautions were taken for his safety. Eventually, however, his good behavior convinced prison authorities to integrate him with the prison population. He was allowed to eat with other inmates and was assigned work details in the prison.

Dahmer was on a work detail on November 28, 1994, with two dangerous inmates. Christopher Scarver, who believed he was the son of God, had been convicted of first-degree murder. Jesse Anderson had murdered his wife. These three men together, given their past crimes, were a deadly combination.

The guards left the three men alone for about twenty minutes, and when they returned, they found Anderson dead and Dahmer lying nearby, still alive but with a crushed

After serving two years at the Columbia Correctional Institute, Dahmer was beaten to death with a broom handle by fellow inmate Christopher Scarver (pictured).

skull. Scarver had attacked both men with a broom handle. Dahmer was pronounced dead a few minutes later.

Notes

Chapter 1: What Is a Serial Killer?

1. Robert K. Ressler, *Whoever Fights Monsters*. New York: St. Martin's Press, 1992, p. 29.

2. Harold Schechter, *The A to Z Encyclopedia of Serial Killers*. New York: Pocket Books, 1996, p. 69.

Chapter 2: The Torture Doctor: H. H. Holmes

3. Harold Schechter, *Depraved*. New York: Pocket Books, 1994, p. 12.

4. Schechter, *Depraved*, pp. 267–68.

5. *New York Times*, "Holmes Cool to the End," July 25, 1895.

6. Quoted in Schechter, *Depraved*, p. 179.

7. Quoted in Schechter, *Depraved*, p. 386.

Chapter 3: The Cannibal Grandpa: Albert Fish

8. Moira Martingale, *Cannibal Killers*. New York: St. Martin's Press, 1993, p. 44.

9. Quoted in Harold Schechter, *Deranged*. New York: Pocket Books, 1990, pp. 230–31.

10. Schechter, *Deranged*, p. 131.

11. *New York Times*, "'Not in Right Mind,' Fish Wrote to Son," March 18, 1935.

12. Quoted in Schechter, *Deranged*, p. 292.

Chapter 4: The Monster That Movies Are Made Of: Ed Gein

13. Harold Schechter, *Deviant*. New York: Pocket Books, 1989, pp. 15–16.

14. Schechter, *Deviant*, p. 80.

Chapter 5: Soviet Stalker: Andrei Chikatilo

15. Richard Lourie, *Hunting the Devil*. New York: HarperCollins, 1993, pp. 6–7.

16. Martingale, *Cannibal Killers*, p. 154.

17. Martingale, *Cannibal Killers*, p. 156.

18. Stephen J. Giannangelo, *The Psychopathology of Serial Murder: A Theory of Violence*. Westport, CT: Praeger, 1996, p. 59.

19. Lourie, *Hunting the Devil,* p. 69.

20. Quoted in Lourie, *Hunting the Devil,* pp. 85–86.

Chapter 6: Killer Clown: John Wayne Gacy

21. Tim Cahill, *Buried Dreams: Inside the Mind of a Serial Killer.* New York: Bantam Books, 1986, p. 46.

22. Rachael Bell, "John Wayne Gacy Jr.," *Dark Horse Crime Library,* http://www.crimelibrary.com/serial/gacy/gacyrumors.htm.

23. Cahill, *Buried Dreams,* p. 96.

24. Michael Newton, *Hunting Humans: An Encyclopedia of Serial Killers.* Port Townsend, WA: Loomponics Unlimited, 1990, p. 120.

25. Cahill, *Buried Dreams,* pp. 195–96.

26. Cahill, *Buried Dreams,* p. 196

27. Cahill, *Buried Dreams,* pp. 231–32.

28. Quoted in Cahill, *Buried Dreams,* p. 257.

29. Michael Cartel, *Disguise of Sanity: Serial Mass Murderers.* Toluca Lake, CA: Pepperbox Books, 1985, p. 202.

30. Quoted in Cahill, *Buried Dreams,* pp. 232–33.

31. Quoted in Robert K. Ressler, *I Have Lived in the Monster.* New York: St. Martin's Press, 1997, p. 94.

32. Cahill, *Buried Dreams,* p. 298.

Chapter 7: Smart and Deadly: Ted Bundy

33. Quoted in Stephen G. Michaud and Hugh Aynesworth, *The Only Living Witness.* New York: Simon and Schuster, 1983, p. 62.

34. Michaud and Aynesworth, *The Only Living Witness,* p. 68.

35. Quoted in Michaud and Aynesworth, *The Only Living Witness,* pp. 76–77.

36. Ann Rule, *The Stranger Beside Me.* New York: W. W. Norton, 1980, p. 62.

37. Quoted in Michaud and Aynesworth, *The Only Living Witness,* pp. 98–99.

38. Cartel, *Disguise of Sanity,* p. 188.

39. Michaud and Aynesworth, *The Only Living Witness,* pp. 227–28.

40. Michaud and Aynesworth, *The Only Living Witness,* p. 240.

41. Michaud and Aynesworth, *The Only Living Witness,* p. 283.

42. Polly Nelson, *Defending the Devil: My Story as Ted Bundy's Last Lawyer*. New York: William Morrow, 1994, pp. 127–28.

Chapter 8: Mild-Mannered Monster: Jeffrey Dahmer

43. Quoted in John Boston, "Jeffrey Dahmer," *Dark Horse Crime Library*, http://www.crimelibrary.com/dahmer/dahmerwhy.htm.

44. Anne Schwartz, *The Man Who Could Not Kill Enough*. New York: Birch Lane Press, 1992, p. 39.

45. Quoted in Ressler, *I Have Lived in the Monster*, p. 113.

46. Quoted in Ressler, *I Have Lived in the Monster*, p. 116.

47. Quoted in Ressler, *I Have Lived in the Monster*, p. 118.

48. Schwartz, *The Man Who Could Not Kill Enough*, p. 50.

49. Quoted in Ressler, *I Have Lived in the Monster*, p. 124.

50. Schwartz, *The Man Who Could Not Kill Enough*, p. 54.

51. Ressler, *Whoever Fights Monsters*, p. 246.

52. Schwartz, *The Man Who Could Not Kill Enough*, p. 10.

53. Schwartz, *The Man Who Could Not Kill Enough*, p. 32.

54. Schwartz, *The Man Who Could Not Kill Enough*, p. 199.

55. Quoted in Schwartz, *The Man Who Could Not Kill Enough*, pp. 216–18.

FOR FURTHER READING

Andrea Campbell, *Forensic Science: Evidence, Clues and Investigation.* New York: Chelsea House, 1999. The author details all aspects of a crime, from the discovery of a crime scene to collecting evidence.

Laura D'Angelo, *The FBI's Most Wanted.* New York: Chelsea House, 1997. A detailed account of the FBI's Most Wanted listing of some of the deadliest criminals in the world.

Robert Dolan, *Serial Murders.* New York: Chelsea House, 1997. This book covers all aspects of serial murder for a young adult audience. Sometimes graphic, it details the various aspects of discovering and solving this kind of crime.

Charlotte Foltz-Jones, *Fingerprints and Talking Bones: How Real-Life Crimes Are Solved.* New York: Bantam Books, 1997. A non-gory book that includes fascinating facts and information on how evidence is used to solve crimes.

Works Consulted

Books

Tim Cahill, *Buried Dreams: Inside the Mind of a Serial Killer.* New York: Bantam Books, 1986. An in-depth account of the life and crimes of John Wayne Gacy.

Michael Cartel, *Disguise of Sanity: Serial Mass Murderers.* Toluca Lake, CA: Pepperbox Books, 1985. A detailed account of serial killers, past and present, and an in-depth look at their crimes.

James Alan Fox and Jack Levin, *Overkill: Mass Murder and Serial Killing Exposed.* New York: Plenum Press, 1994. Fox and Levin's definitive book looks at specific serial killers, such as Ted Bundy, and provides an exhaustive study of the reasons behind their crimes.

Stephen J Giannangelo, *The Psychopathology of Serial Murder: A Theory of Violence.* Westport, CT: Praeger, 1996. A scholarly look at the psychology of some famous serial killers, including Andrei Chikatilo and Jeffrey Dahmer.

Eric W. Hickey, *Serial Murderers and Their Victims.* Belmont, CA: Brooks/Cole Publishing Company, 1991. A scholarly account of various serial killers, including Ted Bundy and John Wayne Gacy, and their crimes. Sections explore how killers choose their victims and the kinds of evidence police look for at the scene of a serial murder.

Ronald M. Holmes, *Profiling Violent Crimes: An Investigative Tool.* London: Sage Publications, 1989. This book, written for crime professionals, details the various aspects of the art of criminal profiling. Areas covered include how to analyze a crime scene and how to successfully profile serial murders, cult murders, and rape.

Richard Lourie, *Hunting the Devil.* New York: HarperCollins, 1993. One of the few comprehensive biographies of Soviet serial killer Andrei Chikatilo, exhaustively researched.

Moira Martingale, *Cannibal Killers.* New York: St. Martin's Press, 1993. A comprehensive survey of serial killers throughout history who ate their victims.

Stephen G. Michaud and Hugh Aynesworth, *The Only Living Witness.* New York: Simon and Schuster, 1983. Two reporters detail the story of Ted Bundy's crimes, based on their interviews with the killer.

Polly Nelson, *Defending the Devil: My Story as Ted Bundy's Last Lawyer.* New York: William Morrow, 1994. A detailed story of the final months of Ted Bundy's life and the behind-the-scenes attempts by his last legal team to save him from execution.

Michael Newton, *Hunting Humans: An Encyclopedia of Modern Serial Killers.* Port Townsend, WA: Loomponics Unlimited, 1990. A meticulous listing of serial killers throughout history and around the world, with brief biographies and overviews of their crimes.

Thomas O'Reilly-Fleming, *Serial and Mass Murder: Theory, Research and Policy.* Toronto: Canadian Scholar's Press, 1996. A team of Canadian researchers delve into aspects of serial murder, including sexual sadism, characteristics of victims, and clinical disorders.

Robert K. Ressler, *I Have Lived in the Monster.* New York: St. Martin's Press, 1997. The famed serial killer expert interviews some of the most famous killers, including John Wayne Gacy and Jeffrey Dahmer.

———, *Whoever Fights Monsters.* New York: St. Martin's Press, 1992. A detailed autobiography of one of the FBI's most respected experts on serial killers and his efforts to capture serial killers around the world.

Ann Rule, *The Stranger Beside Me.* New York: W. W. Norton, 1980. The true account of Ann Rule's friendship with Ted Bundy, from their meeting in 1971 until his execution.

Harold Schechter, *The A to Z Encyclopedia of Serial Killers.* New York: Pocket Books, 1996. An exhaustive listing of all aspects of serial murder, from "animal torture" to "zombies."

———, *Depraved.* New York: Pocket Books, 1994. One of the most thorough accounts of the life of H. H. Holmes, America's first serial killer.

———, *Deranged.* New York: Pocket Books, 1990. The biography of Albert Fish, a killer who terrorized children in the New York area in the early twentieth century.

———, *Deviant.* New York: Pocket Books, 1989. The true account of the life and crimes of Ed Gein, one of America's most notorious killers.

Anne Schwartz, *The Man Who Could Not Kill Enough.* New York: Birch Lane Press, 1992. A detailed biography of Jeffrey Dahmer and an account of his crimes, written by the newspaper reporter who covered the story in 1991.

Periodicals

Gordon Cater, "The Social Construction of the Serial Killer," *RCMP Gazette,* March 1997.

Dana Dettart and John Mahoney, "The Serial Murderer's Motivations: An Interdisciplinary Review," *Omega* 29, no. 1, 1994.

Vernon J. Geberth, "The Serial Killer and the Revelations of Ted Bundy," *Law and Order,* May 1990.

Faith H. Leibman, "Serial Murders: Four Case Histories," *Federal Probation,* December 1989.

Eugene Methvin, "The Face of Evil," *National Review,* January 23, 1995.

New York Times, "Holmes Cool to the End," July 25, 1895.

New York Times, "'Not in Right Mind,' Fish Wrote to Son," March 18, 1935.

Websites

Address: http://www.fbi.gov/programs/vicap/vicap.html. Violent Criminal Apprehension Program and the National Center for the Analysis of Violent Crime (VICAP and NCAVC). An overview of the FBI's programs to apprehend violent criminals.

Address: http://www.crimelibrary.com. *Dark Horse Crime Library.* A series of biographies on the most notorious serial killers, including Albert Fish, Ed Gein, and John Wayne Gacy Jr.

INDEX

Picture Credits

About the Author

Award-winning children's magazine editor and writer Allison Lassieur has published numerous books about history, world cultures, and health. A writer for magazines such as *National Geographic World*, *Highlights for Children*, *Scholastic News*, and *Disney Adventures*, she also writes puzzle books and computer game materials. In addition to writing, Ms. Lassieur studies medieval history. She lives and works in Bucks County, Pennsylvania.